The Legend of

Mary Ellen Dickman

A true story of life in the 20th century starting on a farm in rural Pennsylvania with ten siblings, through the experiences of a life lived to its fullest.

By Mary Ellen Dickman

all the best to –
Dr. Robert Hampton

Mary Ellen Dickman

First Edition

ISBN 978-1721804382

Foreword

The "Legend of Mary Ellen Dickman" is the story of America in the 20th century, much like what the "Little House on The Prairie" story is to the 19th century. Mary is my aunt and I'm inspired by how she lives her life - how she has no fear of trying anything, how neat and clean she is - how she picks up loose papers wherever she goes to keep America beautiful. She recently cleaned up a field and made it into a park, and trims all her neighbors' bushes. She makes the most of her retirement years by living every day with zest and endless energy, always finding new goals and pursuing them, never giving up, never thinking she can't do anything and always believing that something good is about to happen. She puts her faith in God first, and she's a patriot who loves this country.

Having gone through the Great Depression, World War II, and everything since, she has a perspective on the history that shaped our culture. She saw the great leaps forward in technology and industry that brought the average person from mere subsistence to a life of luxury. And in giving us a perspective on life, she also gives us a motivation to be better, to do our best, to strive against all odds and to do things that seem impossible. She became a pilot, an author, an artist, a carpenter, a cook, and many more things, and she executed all she did with excellence. She is relentless, persistent, brave, strong-willed and resolute. She inherited the patriot blood that ran through the veins of her predecessors, those who fought for and formed this country. No doubt she will influence the lives of everyone who reads her story and encourage them too, to be their best.

Cheryl Hefferon, 2018

Meeting Mary Dickman was one of the highlights of my life. One Friday evening on December 1998, I noticed someone moving into the condo next door. My husband and I were hosting a neighborhood party and without hesitation, I ran over to Mary's to introduce myself and immediately I invited her to my party to meet the neighbors. Little did I know by extending the hand of friendship that night, a 20+ year friendship would evolve.

Mary is a pilot, she flew her plane for 25 years. On several occasions, Mary would fly three of her girlfriends (they called themselves the "Plane Janes") to another city for lunch. Mary has numerous talents. She's a tailor, quilter, self-taught organist, oil painter, landscape designer, tree and flower expert, carpenter, she speaks German, and is a gifted author. She likes to gamble on occasion and plays a great game of Scrabble.

As the years passed, Mary and I got closer. If I didn't see her at least once a week, I'd have withdrawal. She's my confidant, my voice of reason, my best friend, and an all-around nice person. I thank God for putting Mary in my life. She has taught me so much and I would not be the same without her. I love her dearly and have been enriched by her friendship. Her book is just like her, delightful and full of surprises.

Kathy Sassano, 2018

A special Thank You to those who helped me author this book:

Deanna Adams - Author
Debra Muzik - Instructor
Christina Porter - Author
Cheryl Hefferon who published it for me

To Touch an Eagle

By Nancy Stock

An Eagle comes
from the place in your mind
where "free" is more than a word.
Where "flight"
is a feeling that floats on the wind
like the wings of a golden bird.
Somewhere deep
within my soul
I felt an Eagle grow
When landing gear released me
from the world I used to know,
And wide wings let me pioneer
a continent of space
Where rays
of Heaven's sunlight
wait to warm an earthly face.
The spirit of the Eagle beckoned
just beyond my reach;
I followed it to practice grounds
above a silver beach.
And, searching for perfection
over miles of mirrored sea,
I studied the reflection
of a world yet strange to me.
A world that holds
an Eagle's touch
somewhere in skies unknown,
A field of silver,

gold and blue
where cotton clouds are sown.
With the essence of an Eagle
And a teacher's patient hand
I found a place
for boundless dreams
above a patchwork land.
My heart found room
for soaring
where no pilot ever flew.
One substance were
my plane and I,
one being made from two.
And though I'll cross
A million skies
before I reach my goal,
I'll treasure moments
when I know
I've touched an Eagle's soul!

Contents

Chapter 1 - My Life

This is the story of a journey through life from 1927 to 2018 and beyond. I have learned that many things are possible if you believe in yourself, exert the energy and have the will. Despite the occasional storms, life can be very enjoyable.

Growing up the way I did didn't seem so difficult because I had nothing to compare it to. What you get used to seems normal. Looking back, I wouldn't change anything, because it worked for me and my siblings. I made some good decisions and a few bad ones. This is how we learn. My parents must have had some sleepless nights, being responsible for so many things and for such a large family. Prayers helped us through it all.

I want to dedicate this book to my family and friends and hope they enjoy reading it. They were with me through much of it, which helped me accomplish more later in life. In the eyes of many people, I would not be considered a success, but if what you accomplish makes you feel good about yourself, then I would say that is being successful.

Chapter 2 - Buying the Farm

It's hard for people living in the middle of today's technology to imagine growing up on a farm with absolutely no conveniences, not even running water. But that was my childhood. It was challenging, rewarding and always exciting. I learned fast that growing up the seventh child of ten doesn't allow for much special attention, so I was a quiet, bashful girl. But there were other lessons I learned, too, that molded me into a daring, independent woman who wasn't afraid to try something new. I learned to be like my parents and do what had to be done to survive, and I learned I had to always grow and do different things to keep life's journey from being dull.

My father, Frank Frederick, was the son of Samuel and Mary Himes Frederick. He had one brother and one sister. He left home when he was 18 and worked his way out west but then he made his way back to his parents' home.

My mother, Sarah Swisher, lived in Clairton, Pennsylvania. She had three brothers and one sister. Her childhood was tragic – her father died, and because there was no government assistance for families back then, her mother had to take in laundry to feed the family. She couldn't earn enough to support them all, though, so my mother had to go and live with an aunt and uncle in Sprankle Mills, Pennsylvania, and two of her brothers went to live with a different family.

Frank Frederick and Sarah Swisher were married May 11, 1915 when he was 25 and she was 23. They had ten children. I was the seventh. An eleventh child, a son, died during birth soon after we moved to our family farm in Punxsutawney, Pennsylvania.

I was born at my grandparents' home in Sprankle Mills. My parents hadn't named me yet when the doctor recorded

2

my birth, so my birth certificate had a blank for the first name and Frederick for the last for years. When my father was getting old, I realized I had better get his signature on a form so I could get a legal birth certificate, which I did.

My earliest memories are when my family lived temporarily with my father's parents in Sprankle Mills. Our living there must have been a huge inconvenience for my grandparents, but I never heard an angry word spoken, except when Grandmother complained about Grandfather going fishing when there was so much work to be done. Grandfather Frederick was six feet tall and spoke slowly with a heavy German accent. Grandmother was a small woman but had a lot of control over absolutely everything. One thing I remember about her was that she handed out a lot of soda crackers to us kids. My youngest brother, James, was born there during the time we were staying with my grandparents. My Dad always worked while we were there, among other jobs, on a drilling rig.

I don't know who taught me, but by the time I was 4, I knew the alphabet and numbers. Because of that, my parents decided to send me to school with my brothers and sisters. I was too shy to talk. The teacher was very patient with me, she tried treats, coaxing, but it didn't work. She couldn't get me to talk. In an attempt to get me to speak, I was told I could sit with anyone in the class and I chose David Coulter, who had a sheepskin lined coat on his seat, but I still wouldn't talk. My parents decided to wait until the next year to send me to school. From March through September, 1932, my brothers and sisters kept telling me that once I went to first grade, I would definitely have to talk.

The farm was pretty self-sufficient. They had a springhouse close to the house and a very cold natural spring supplied the water. A springhouse is a small building that is built over a natural spring of water. Out in the country, you are on your own for water and most often the water supply determines the location where the home is built. They kept a trough filled with the cold spring water to help preserve food. There was a gas well on the farm so they had free heat and gas lights in the house. There was an outdoor clay oven where Grandmother baked bread and an in-ground pit where they kept potatoes, carrots, onions, apples and pumpkins in the winter. I remember the stairway to the second floor of the house where Grandmother had a cloth bag of dried fruit and a container of oatmeal. In the parlor there was a leather chair and a large leather couch with a bear skin on the back of it. There was also an organ with two mounted pheasants sitting on top.

I remember the day my grandparents took me to get my smallpox vaccination. Afterwards, we went to the house of relatives Roy and Annie Dobson, and they made popcorn. I also have a clear memory of the day in the barnyard when a big rooster knocked me down. My grandfather heard me cry out and rescued me. Another time, I went to the outdoor toilet and while I was in there, it started raining very hard. I waited a while but it didn't stop so I got soaked running back to the house. I burst into the house crying and Grandfather sat down in a rocking chair, gathered me into his lap and I fell asleep. When I woke up, I was still in his lap and I felt very safe and loved.

One of my favorite places on the farm was sitting way up in the black cherry tree where I could be by myself and eat cherries. I still love to climb trees.

Meanwhile, my father was looking for a large farm where he could rear his family and he found it in Punxsutawney, Pennsylvania when I was 5 years old. We moved there in March of 1932. The farm was owned by Peter Lott Brown, who was president of the Punxsutawney National Bank. The people who lived on the farm before us were not industrious people and the property was not a pretty sight. The buildings needed repairs and the surrounding areas were grown over with weeds and brush.

It was an eight-room house with 10' ceilings downstairs and 9' ceilings upstairs. There were fireplaces in three rooms downstairs and in three rooms upstairs, and there was a coal furnace in the basement, but only one large register at the bottom of the stairs in front of the front door.

There was no electricity in the house. We used kerosene lamps and lanterns for light. There was no water inside, either, but we had a very good spring with constantly running water that went into a wooden barrel at the edge of the back porch. Snakes liked to lay on the wet stones by the barrel and anytime my mother saw one, she would say, "Get the hoe" and that snake would be killed fast. Water was piped through the basement wall into a cement trough where we kept butter, cream, milk and anything else we didn't want to spoil.

It was cold and dreary the day we moved in and I was told that I took one look at that poor, glum farmhouse and cried, saying I didn't want to stay there – that I wanted to go to Mum's house, meaning my grandparents' house.

It was very swampy on three sides of the house and a lot of willows grew there. Dad and my brothers Floyd and Lee worked very hard clearing and draining that area to make room for gardens. Dad had to buy horses and machinery to do the farming and they farmed that way for a number of years before we bought a red Farmall tractor and then, eventually, a green John Deere tractor. One day when we still used horses, I was sent to the field to tell my brother Floyd that it was time for lunch and he let me ride on the back of one of the horses. That day I learned that farm horses are very big and not for riding.

There was a small creek running close to the house that we used to irrigate the garden and we were rewarded with

5

beautiful heads of iceberg lettuce, pascal celery, Chinese cabbage, onions, carrots and beets. We also grew rhubarb, Swiss chard, tomatoes, peppers, cucumbers, cauliflower, broccoli, watermelon, cantaloupe and eggplant. We had a separate potato garden, red and black raspberries and a long strawberry patch. We had apple, peach and pear trees and a butternut tree.

We had several sweet corn fields, planted at different times so they didn't all get ripe at once. Fresh corn is sweeter than corn sitting in the store for days, so as soon as the first corn was ripe, people would come from Punxsutawney to buy a couple dozen ears of corn. Whenever someone came to buy corn, whoever was available would run to the field and pick as many ears as the customer wanted. It could be anywhere from one dozen to six or eight. It doesn't get fresher than that. Of course my father also took corn to the farmers market and sold some to a market in town.

The girls' bedroom had two double beds in it and the two older boys' room had a double bed. My parents' room had two double beds, one for them and one for the three younger boys. Once they got older, the boys moved into the fourth bedroom.

We started to redeem the house by tearing off the old wallpaper and my parents and older sisters found a big surprise under the wallpaper – bedbugs in the corner that was warmed by the chimney going up through. After we took care of the bugs, the beautiful woodwork in the house had to be washed and varnished.

There was a coal cook stove in the kitchen and we used the fireplace in the living room for heat until my father bought a larger heater that burned wood or coal. We girls used the fireplace in our bedroom several times when we had friends over. It was so pleasant to sit and talk in front of the crackling fire. In the winter when it was really cold, you could see your breath in the house and there was frost on the insides of the windows. We snuggled for warmth under very heavy quilts and comforters at night.

It was almost a year before we got electricity in the house, but it was a relief when we did. The oil lamps and lanterns were terribly inconvenient and very unsafe. We had an outside toilet but for the young children there was a pot in the area at the top of the stairs so we wouldn't have to go out into the cold darkness in the middle of the night. One night I got up to use the pot, and being half asleep, sat on the hot lantern instead. I screamed loud enough to wake everyone in the house. Mother and Dad got up and put Vicks VapoRub on my poor burnt butt. Vicks was the remedy for a lot of things in those days.

This will sound pretty gross, but since money was scarce and we didn't buy anything that wasn't absolutely necessary, in the outside toilet we used catalogs instead of toilet tissue. There was Sears Roebuck, J.C. Penney's and Aldens. Every season they supplied us with new catalogs, so there was no problem having paper handy.

P.L. Brown was still the owner of the farm and for payment of rent, we sharecropped and he received a percentage of profits from crops and was supplied fresh meat from butchered cows, pigs and chickens. He also got fresh vegetables all summer long.

Dad built our toys for us. We had a wooden bobsled that we would take high up on a hill and ride down, a wagon with wooden wheels and wooden stilts we could walk on like clowns did. We had no roller skates or bikes – there would have been no place to use them on the farm. When the creek froze over, we didn't have skates so we would just skate on it with our shoes.

We did have a large wooden game board for playing checkers, and later got a game of Chinese checkers. We had a deck of author cards, which I especially liked. Edgar Allen Poe, Charles Dickens, Alfred Lord Tennyson and others.

During the depression, times were bad for poor people. Franklin Roosevelt was president. He started W.P.A. and C.C.C. The W.P.A. provided construction and road work jobs. They built a very nice cement bridge in front of our house over Jackson Run. It had been an old wooden bridge. The C.C.C. was for young men. They had camps and worked in forestry.

The Countryside that stretched from Punxsutawney to Sprankle Mills was very mountainous and hilly. Roads were cut through hills which left high banks on either side. County road workers had planted vetch to prevent erosion of the dirt that would have come down on the highway. Vetch had pretty lavender flowers which made a pleasant view on the way to visit relatives in the summer and early fall. Things like this make fond memories.

A Bit of Cuteness…

When I was 3 years old I had a blue coat. My mother told me that I called it "my little blue little coat."

When I was 6 and my brother Bob was 4, we spent a day at my oldest sister's mother-in-law's place. She was keeping an eye on us. Bob fell off the porch and started crying. I helped him up, brushed him off and said, "Don't cry, Bobbie. Be tough."

I can't tell you how many times I heard that phrase repeated by Mrs. Zufall.

8

Chapter 3 - My Siblings

I am number seven in the Frederick family. Being the only one still living from a family of ten has compelled me to write my biography. I loved each and every one of my siblings for who they were and the impact they had in my life.

The older boys liked to play tricks on some of us younger kids. In the winter they would give us a burlap bag and send us out in the snow to hunt snipes. We would get very cold waiting for one to come along. Of course, we eventually discovered that snipes don't exist.

We all turned into good people because of how we were raised. We didn't get a lot of orders or demands. We weren't allowed to fight with each other or use bad words. We were threatened with soap in our mouth if we did. We were taught honesty and loyalty by example.

Since there are a lot of us to keep straight, here's a little biography on each of my siblings. They are listed oldest to youngest.

Hazel

Hazel was my oldest sister. She had brown eyes and medium brown hair with some natural curl. She was 5'6" tall. Hazel was 16 when we moved to the farm. She began dating Joseph Zufall, who lived about a mile away in Cloe. Joseph appeared to be irresponsible because he had the habit of driving past our house very fast to show off for Hazel. Hazel and Joseph eloped suddenly one day and were married. My parents were extremely upset; my mother even collapsed and fell to the floor when she found out.

Hazel and Joseph lived in an old farmhouse for a time and that's where their daughter was born. Hazel and Joseph then moved to Niagara Falls where Joseph worked in a carborundum plant. In the following years three sons were born to them: Joseph, Frederick and Larry. The family returned to Cloe when Joseph's mother became ill and they moved in with her and Joseph's father.

Hazel had only gone through eighth grade in school. She was right at home on the farm, milking cows, taking care of the milk and making butter. She had a large garden and she canned fruit and vegetables and baked bread. She cut her family's hair and made their clothes and built a stone fireplace in the living room. She also helped lay the hardwood floors in the dining and sun rooms. Hazel grew beautiful flowers and had a lemon and an orange tree growing in the sun room.

Hazel always had a positive attitude and I very much enjoyed being with her. Once when I was 10 years old, Hazel had me babysit so she could go out and work in the garden. Her baby girl, Nancy, was on the table where I was changing her diaper. I turned away for just a second to get baby oil and she rolled off the table onto the floor. I was very scared but Nancy wasn't hurt. She is over 80 today.

Hazel had a stroke and passed away at the age of 73. Joseph passed from cancer at age 82.

Floyd

Floyd was my oldest brother. He was 5'11" tall and had grey eyes and reddish-brown hair with a small amount of natural curl. Floyd was never loud. He kept busy, especially loved sweets, and couldn't get enough of working on mechanical things. He only finished eighth grade in school but became an excellent mechanic. When I was 11 or 12, Floyd liked to call me "freckle face" which I didn't particularly like.

But once again, that nickname was something I could call mine and mine alone.

Floyd worked on the farm until he married Violet Fenstemaker, a tall woman who laughed often. They had one daughter and three sons.

Floyd worked a few different jobs before he was hired on at the steel mill in Aliquippa, Pennsylvania. He worked there until he retired. His hobby was buying old tractors and rebuilding the engines. One year he even entered one in a county fair.

Violet loved to cook. She passed away after having a stroke when she was 72.

Floyd fell to bone cancer and passed away when he was 86.

Lee

Lee was the second son in the Frederick family. He was 5'10" tall. He had brown eyes, very curly brown hair, a good sense of humor and he loved to tease. When he was in his teens he and a friend went to the woods one night and caught an opossum. He brought it in the house and chased me around the kitchen with it. I still dislike opossums to this day.

Lee pulled a trick on me at our grandparents' house when I was 7 and he was 14. We were on the sidewalk between the back porch and the springhouse. A couple other siblings were there also. There was a distance between us and Lee told me to come over to him. I was in my bare feet and as I walked toward him I stepped on a house snake that was stretched across the sidewalk. I didn't see it because the color of the snake almost blended into the color of the cement. It scared me so badly that I got chills up my spine and I said a bad word.

Of course, they all laughed and Lee said, "Uh, oh I'm going to tell Mom."

Lee started his freshman year in high school but quit, saying he didn't have nice enough clothes to wear to school. He worked on the farm until he was 18 and then joined the Army. When my brother Lee came home from the Army after 4 years, he was entitled to some free education through the GI bill. He chose to learn how to fly and got his pilot license, but he didn't do much flying after that.

One time my husband Jay and I flew to Punxsutawney to visit relatives. Lee and Helen and Jay and I went to the airport and I took my brother for an airplane ride. I think he truly enjoyed having his little sister take him for a ride.

Lee was at home for a while until he married Helen Lydic. They helped our parents on the farm for a while and then tried a couple of different jobs. When my mother passed from cancer, Dad sold the farm to Lee.

Later, Lee was repairing the barn roof when he fell off and broke an arm and a leg. The leg got infected and took a long time to heal.

Lee and Helen had one daughter and one son. Lee built a log cabin for their daughter and her husband. He loved working with wood and built new cabinets in the kitchen at the farmhouse.

Helen was a hairdresser and worked at a local beauty shop.

Lee passed away of lung disease at age 85.

Helen is presently living in Punxsutawney, Pennsylvania.

Kathryn

Kathryn was the second daughter in the Frederick family. She was 5'9" tall, had brown eyes and dark brown hair with natural curl. She was kind and considerate of others. We called her Kay.

After my sister Hazel left home, I slept with Kay. I was 6 years old and I wet the bed one night. It was cold and I was sitting up in bed crying. Kay woke up and very gently said, "Don't cry. I'll get a dry blanket." I'll always remember that she was so patient with me and careful not to make me feel worse than I already did.

Kay liked playing the harmonica. She went to high school for 3 years and then worked as a housemaid in a family home for a year to save some money for school and graduation expenses. When she had saved enough, she went back to school and finished her fourth year.

Kay and my other sister, June, worked at the hospital as nurse's aides. Later they went to Niagara Falls and stayed temporarily with Joe and Hazel Zufall while they worked in a corset factory.

Kay dated Wilson Blair, who was in the Army. When he came home, they got married.

Kay was always generous with me. She made a couple of cotton tops and a skirt for me and when I got married, she bought me a set of dishes.

When my husband Fred and I were living in Youngstown, Ohio, we went to Punxsutawney once a month. Several times, I had Kay give me a haircut while we were there.

Kay and Wilson had one son and one daughter. The son, William, was 7 years old and the daughter, Mary Lynda, was 3 years old when Kay passed away from a brain tumor at the young age of 31. Wilson later married Ann London and together they added more children to their family.

June

June was the third daughter in the Frederick family. She was 5'9" tall. She had brown eyes and very curly brown hair. She was really fast at picking berries, beans and peas in the garden. When I was about 12 years old, I was thrilled that June curled my hair with a curling iron several times.

June quit high school in her freshman year because, after getting scarlet fever and missing a lot of school, she got behind in the lessons and was discouraged. She got a job as a housemaid for a family in Punxsutawney. Later she got a job at an ice cream parlor/restaurant.

After Kay graduated, she and June went to Niagara Falls to work. I went to visit them and June took me shopping and bought a beautiful dress for me. I then stayed a week with Joe and Hazel Zufall.

June dated a man for a couple of years and then met Lawrence Rose, who she married. June and Larry had one daughter and one son. Larry worked at the Nabisco Shredded Wheat factory. While the family was on a long-planned vacation, Larry got very sick. He was later diagnosed with lung cancer and passed away when their son, Danny, was 7 years old.

June worked in a restaurant for many years and then started working as a companion for wealthy old ladies.

June and their daughter Cheryl formed a clown program to entertain children and older people who were in hospitals and care homes. June had a great sense of humor and could remember poems, rhymes and jokes. June was an excellent seamstress and she loved growing flowers. June passed away at the age of 93.

Ruth

Ruth was my fourth sister and my best friend ever. She was 2 years older than I and I was allowed to go a lot of places if I was with her that I wouldn't have been permitted to go to alone. Ruth was 5'6" tall. She had brown eyes and light brown curly hair.

Ruth was the only one who would tease at our Mother by saying she was going on a trip (on a slow boat to China). I always laughed although I don't know where that expression came from.

Ruth quit school in her junior year of high school. She went to Niagara Falls and got a job in the meat department of a grocery store.

Ruth had been dating Glenn Smith, who was in the Army. When he was discharged she came back to Punxsutawney and they were married. Ruth and Glenn had two daughters and one son. They moved several times because of Glenn's job working on cement highway construction.

When her son Richard was 9 years old, Ruth studied and took the high school equivalency, or GED test. After she passed that, she began nursing school and after graduating, worked as a practical nurse for 12 years.

Ruth and Glenn moved to Florida and lived there for several years until they moved back to Silver Creek, New York, to be closer to family. While Ruth was in Cleveland for treatment of a bowel disorder, she fell, broke her leg, and never got back home.

Ruth passed away at age 73. Glenn Smith passed away two weeks later at the age of 74. They always had many friends and Glenn loved to throw parties.

Mary

I am the seventh Frederick child. I am 5' tall now, although I used to be 5'2" at my tallest. I am the only one in the family who had blonde hair and green eyes.

There was a family portrait taken long before I was born, but only a snapshot of family members taken when I was three years old.

My father called me "Runt" as a nickname because I was so small. Although it isn't a very complimentary term, I admit that I enjoyed him having a special name just for me.

I've made many items of clothing and quilts and I've crocheted nine afghans. I taught myself to play the organ. I took classes to learn oil painting. I learned to fly and became a pilot. I love gardening and growing beautiful flowers.

I loved watching my father build things from wood when I was a child. I liked the smell and watching the little curls of wood shavings that came off as he used the planer. After I retired, I built two saw horses. Later I refinished a buffet, built a park bench and three small tables to hold flower pots.

In 2006, I built two pairs of stilts for my granddaughter Alison and her friend. They had fun walking on them.

I love playing Scrabble with family members and with my friend of 20 years, Kathy Sassano.

I dream every night, and mostly have at least two dreams. I write them down in a notebook and have filled many notebooks with my dreams.

I dearly love horses. I could watch them all day. They are so graceful and beautiful when they walk and run. I enjoy going to fairs to watch the horse contests. I would have owned one if it had been feasible.

I am fascinated by cloud formations and beautiful skies and have taken many pictures. I have four albums filled with sky pictures. I also love beautiful leaves. I gather and press them in the fall and often put them in picture frames to give away as gifts.

Robert

Robert was number eight, the third brother in my family. We called him Bob. He was 5'11" tall. He had brown eyes and straight brown hair as a child. When Bob was an adult, his hair became so curly he actually would have the barber thin his hair.

Bob decided against going to high school. He worked at home on the farm until he was old enough to join the Air Force. He and a school friend joined together. When Bob was at home on leave he met Norma Fetterman. He was telling me about her and I could see he was in love. They were married and moved to Buffalo, New York. Bob finished his education in the Air Force, then continued classes and was hired as a result of his education. He became head engineer of Convair Aircraft Corporation in San Diego, California. Bob continued taking classes for many years and college became a way of life for him.

Bob and Norma had no children but Bob took up the hobby of making wooden toys for children. He had a complete woodworking shop and joined a group of woodworkers.

Norma worked in personnel at a knife factory. She had a very large doll collection.

Bob passed away from a heart attack when he was 75 years old.

At present, Norma is still living in San Diego.

Richard

Richard is number nine in the Frederick family, brother number four. We called him Richie when he was a child, but when he got older he liked to be called Dick. Dick was 5'8" tall. He had brown eyes and light brown curly hair. He seemed very disciplined and serious and seemed to always be busy or thinking about something.

Dick showed an interest in music when he was young. In his early teens he took violin lessons from Joseph Zufall Sr., our sister Hazel's father-in-law. Dick was the one brother who graduated from high school. After high school, Dick went to piano tuning school in Harrisburg, Pennsylvania.

Dick loved working with wood. He made a violin and a mandolin by cutting, whittling and sanding the wood. He also loved having a garden.

Dick joined the Navy and was in for 4 years. When he came home, he married LaRue Pierce. Dick and LaRue had five children: two daughters and three sons. Dick and LaRue lived in Parsippany, New Jersey for a few years and then moved to Fort Collins, Colorado, where Dick was a piano and organ tuner. He loved his work.

Dick passed away from cancer at age 84.

LaRue is still residing in Fort Collins, Colorado.

James

James was the fifth son and the youngest in the family of ten. Jim, as we called him, was 5'9" tall. He had brown eyes and brown hair with a slight curl. Jim went to high school for one year and played bass in the band. He worked on the farm until he married Mary Gear. They started with twin boys and then had two more boys. Jim and Mary were divorced, then

Jim went to Parsippany, New Jersey to work. Jim met and married Barbara Broadfoot and they had two daughters.

Jim was an active member of the New Jersey Wood Turner's Association. He was a truck driver for a soft drink company, delivering to stores. He always had a very productive vegetable garden. He made many wooden objects: goblets, bowls, glasses, pens and foot stools.

Jim passed away from bone cancer at the age of 82.

Barbara still resides in Parsippany, New Jersey.

Chapter 4 - School Days

We went to a one room schoolhouse that had grades 1 through 8. There was no kindergarten. As much as I enjoyed summers, I thought about starting school all summer long and couldn't wait. It was a mile walk. Our teacher, Mary Schwab was young, pretty and very nice. The first year went just fine but then Miss Schwab said she was leaving and wouldn't be at our school in the fall. She came by our house during the summer and took me shopping. She bought me a pretty yellow dress and socks, a coloring book, cut out dolls and candy. I still have the dress.

Country School teachers truly earned their pay because besides teaching all eight grades, they had to make the fire, clean the school and make sure there was water to drink.

Grace Smouse was my friend in grade school. We played jacks at lunchtime. In nice weather we played soft ball and other games in the yard. When there was snow we slid down the hill on boards.

Two of my closest girlfriends lived less than an eighth of a mile from our home. The dividing line for schools was between our homes so I went to Bell School and they went to Cloe School. Later, we did all go to the same high school.

When I was in fourth grade, I especially liked Wayne Hartfeld. When we played games in the schoolyard and I got near him, I liked that he always smelled of soap. He had a bicycle and he let me ride it a couple of times over the summer. I never had a bicycle of my own until I was 65.

I became the protector of my three younger brothers and often had to rush them along so we wouldn't be late for school. In the morning I packed our lunches and made sure the boys washed up. Before we left I would comb their hair.

We walked the mile to school in all kinds of weather. In winter the snow would get very deep and difficult for very short legs to wade through. They wouldn't plow the secondary roads like ours, until all the main roads were plowed. At home we would play outdoors in the snow until our hands and feet got so cold, we would have to go in. The effects of having my hands and feet frozen are still with me.

There were wild strawberries and teaberries growing along the road and sometimes we picked them on the way to and from school. One time a delivery truck passing by the grade school lost a couple crates of eggs. Some of the older students went down and retrieved several dozen. Our teacher, Miss McConnel, boiled them on top of the potbelly coal heated stove. It had a flat top and she cooked enough so that we each got at least one egg.

There was a store called the Trading Post and Service Station, which was about one tenth of a mile away. The teacher sent Gerald Maruca, an older student, to the store to buy some salt to put on the eggs. They were very good, and it was a lot of fun, especially considering how we got them.

When Kay was in seventh grade at Bell School, she was late getting to school one morning. Our teacher, Mr. Pifer, asked her why she was late and she said, "Because I didn't get here on time." He smiled but made no comment. Kay was lucky. I remember the time Mr. Pifer went to his car and got a rubber hose to keep the older boys in line.

The family that lived on the farm next to ours had eight children. I walked to school with the Wachob boys and I liked Harry best, but one time I caught him and washed his face with snow. I knew I shouldn't have done that and felt bad afterwards. I walked with Ed most of the time because he was a talker and I was a listener.

My sister Ruth and I spent a lot of time with the Wachob boys. Once when we were at their house, we were out in the barn. Ruth ran into the edge of the door with her hand and broke her wrist. Her hand was bent straight over and she just pulled it back up with her other hand. She didn't want our parents to know she broke her wrist so I didn't tell. She told everyone it was sprained to explain it being bandaged. The only lucky part is that she was left handed and it was her right wrist that was broken. She went to school with her arm in a sling and suffered through some terrible pain. That wrist was crooked for the rest of her life.

Once we had passed eighth grade, we had to take final examinations to determine if we were permitted to go to high school. The test was tough and it took nearly all day.

I believe I inherited my mother's quiet demeanor. My extreme shyness caused me discomfort through my teens and beyond. I couldn't speak in front of a group of people.

When I was in my second year of High School, in my English 2 class, I was scheduled to give an oral presentation of an article I had read. I stayed at home that day to avoid having to do it. The next day when I came to class, Miss Gibson asked me to stand up and recite what I had read. I got up and stood there frozen with my red face throbbing. I couldn't say for sure, but I don't think I said anything, because I remember Miss Gibson saying, "You can sit down Mary". If I had given the topic, I would have naturally sat down when I was through. My classmates didn't say anything that I heard about, and I was too embarrassed to ask anyone.

I gained self-confidence gradually over the years. Anyone who has never been shy can't understand the feeling it causes.

I received quite good grades in English 2. They were better than the grades in English 1 by Miss Coleman and her Classic Literature.

I took Homemaking class each of the four years in high school. I decided that no matter what I did in life, there were certain things I would need to know. When I was 16 I began baking pies at home. My parents were very impressed.

Ruth and I spent a lot of time together until she was 16 and she got a new girlfriend. I had three friends my age I began to hang out with – Betty Jane, Nora Jane and Clara Jane. It was almost enough to make me consider calling myself Mary Jane instead of Mary Ellen.

In high school I had dates with several different young men. In my senior year I began going steady with Leonard Emberg. He was Swedish and his nickname was Swede. We broke up when he joined the Navy and then I dated Raymond Mohney for over a year. Raymond was 6' tall and a very nice-looking gentleman.

I was 17 when I graduated from high school. My four sisters went together and bought a beautiful Benrus wrist watch for me. It was pink gold and I used it for over 30 years.

I would have liked to go to college but didn't have the money and I was too timid to consider leaving home and working to finance my education. I was through school and still at home when Mother got the mumps. She stayed in bed upstairs and I took over the cooking and cleaning. She got upset every time I brought up a pan or a meal because I hadn't had the mumps, but I didn't catch them then and still haven't.

Being the last girl at home, I felt needed, but I knew, at age 19, that I had to do something. I got a job as a waitress at Raffetto's Restaurant. It didn't take long for me to know this wasn't what I wanted to do. I worked there six weeks then got a job at Sylvania in Brookville, which was thirty miles away. I worked 3 to 11 p.m. and rode a bus that got back to Punxsutawney near midnight. Sometimes I met with some friends at an all-night restaurant, usually until 1 a.m.

Chapter 5 - Life on the Farm

The duties of farm living are never ending. I believe it takes a lot of faith to be a farmer. There are times when there isn't enough rain and others when it rains too much. Sometimes it isn't warm enough for the crops to grow and at others the frost would come after the crops had started to grow so they had to be replanted. Occasionally my father would remind us to keep the faith by bellowing out a verse of his favorite hymn, "When the roll is called up yonder, I'll be there." We attended the Methodist church in Cloe. My parents were good people and good examples for their children. I never heard them have a loud disagreement. If they had any arguments, they must have taken place in private.

Our farmhouse had a large kitchen with an adjoining pantry that had built in, wall to wall cupboards. There was a sink in the pantry but no running water. In the kitchen there was a large china cabinet that my father built.

We had a very long dining table with a bench on each side. My father sat at the end of the table and my oldest brother, Floyd, sat to his left. Then sat Lee, then Mary, then Ruth, and then June at the end on a chair. On the other side was Kay, Bob, Dick, Jim and then Mother sat on a chair to the right of my father.

Mealtimes were always peaceful. Father would ask the blessing – the same one every time: "Our Heavenly Father, we thank thee that thou has permitted us to sit around this table spread with the necessary comfort of life. Bless this food before us and thank you for its intended use for our bodies. In Jesus' name. Amen."

Sometimes at dinner Dad would tell a story about something he did in the past. Mother cooked three meals a day but she was very quiet and seldom said anything. She was accomplished in many different ways. She cooked, baked bread, made butter, made clothes, quilted, braided rugs, mended, and canned fruits, vegetables and meats. We could work side by side with her for hours and not say one single word.

Mother never owned a pair of slacks nor flat heeled shoes. She always wore dresses, nylon hose and shoes with two-inch heels, no matter what she was doing.

We had a coal stove in the kitchen for cooking and sometimes we would peel and slice potatoes and bake them right on the stove top. Those were our potato chips -- we never had store bought ones. Sometimes we popped corn on the stove in a big metal popper that Dad made.

It was a wonderful treat when we got a radio. When we came home from school we would sit on the floor in front of the radio and listen to our favorite programs. I remember Tom Mix, Jack Armstrong and Roy Rodgers. On Saturday evenings, we listened to good comedy like Bob Hope, Fred Allen, Jack Benny and Hee-Haw.

My father was always a Republican. He listened to political speeches on the radio and I often listened with him. My father would cut our neighbor Bill Hartzfeld's hair and when he came over, they would discuss politics. They often disagreed because Bill was a Democrat. In later years, my dad called President Carter Peanut Carter because he owned a peanut farm and because he didn't agree with his policies of governing.

Later, we got a telephone. The phone had a party line we shared with a neighbor. There was one ring if the call was for the neighbor and two rings if the call was for us.

My mother always wore an apron that had many uses. She used it for wiping tears, drying hands, carrying vegetables from the garden and much more.

Washing and ironing was serious work. Clothes were not easy to come by so it was necessary to take care of the clothes we had. My mother made my three younger brothers' shirts and one year she made six of them, two each. I was around 13 when I sewed all the buttons on and made the buttonholes. Mom also made quilts, comforters and braided rugs.

We did our laundry in a metal tub with a scrub board. We carried the spring water from the barrel at the edge of the porch in to the kitchen coal stove and heated it in a large copper boiler. Sometime after we got electricity in the house, we got a washing machine. Ironing was difficult. We had three irons that fit on a holder with a wooden handle that were heated on the coal stove. When one iron cooled off too much, we changed irons. We starched the clothes and sprinkled them with water.

I never remember my mother telling jokes or saying anything that could be taken as humor, but she had to have had a sense of humor to raise ten kids. Once when she was getting plates out of the cupboard she said, "These plates are wet." I had dried them so I said, "They must be sweating." She gave me a slight grin – the closest she had to a laugh – but didn't say a word. We had so many dishes to dry that the dish towel would get wet before we were through.

When we were young, especially in the winter, my father would get up first and start breakfast. He would make buckwheat cakes and sausages, or pancakes and bacon. Occasionally, he would make oatmeal.

When it was nine o'clock, dad would say, in a raised voice "It's bedtime, kids", and we would go upstairs to bed. In the morning when it was time to get up, from the bottom of the stairs, dad would call out in a loud voice, "Girls!" A little later he would call out "Boys!" We knew we had to get up. No individual names, just Girls and Boys.

To accommodate his large family, Dad bought seven passenger cars. He bought used ones and I remember two different Packards and a Cadillac. Ruth learned to drive in the Cadillac when she was 16. Lee had a black Studebaker Rockne when he was in his teens. It was a sharp looking car that had been named for celebrated football coach Knute Rockne. Floyd had a maroon Buick touring car with eising glass windows. Eising was a type of vinyl or plastic used in the place of glass. Floyd was nice about taking us for rides. When I learned to drive at age 18, we had a five passenger Ford I practiced in. I also got to drive Floyd and Lee's cars while I was learning. It was easy enough to get access to a car since we didn't lock our house or car doors, and the car keys were always kept handy right in the cars. Yet, we never touched anyone else's car unless we had permission from them to do so.

On holidays we would go to visit Grandpa Frederick and at other times we would go to Aunt Lizzie's or Uncle Bill's. Sometimes relatives came to our house for dinner. Dad always asked the blessing at meals and said the same one he recited every time for our family meals at home.

We had an organ and Mom used to play. Later, Dad got her a piano and she would play while some of us sang. In her teens, Kay had a harmonica. Dick and Jim loved music. For a while Dick, Jim, Joe Zufall and Louie Stiver would get together to play music.

We all worked in the garden as soon as we were old enough. We planted, weeded and picked. We had very good gardens and sold some vegetables at the market. We always had good food and plenty of it. Mom canned vegetables, fruits and meat. We raised cows, pigs and chickens. Mom made bread and we made our own butter. We all took our turn milking the cows. I milked every day until I started going to high school.

Sometimes on Saturday Dad would come home with a big box of bananas. The stores were closed Sundays and the bananas would be too ripe by Monday so he got a good price. Sometimes he also bought us some candy on Saturdays.

We kids cleared the rocks out of the creek to make a dam so it would be deep enough to swim in. It was cold! There were willows growing at the edge of the creek and sometimes we would have to chase snakes out of them. We used to catch minnows and little bullheads in the run by the bridge where it wasn't very deep. There was a beautiful dam about a half mile up the hill but we smaller kids weren't allowed to go there unless an older brother or sister went along.

The men went rabbit hunting in the fall and sometimes our mother's brothers, Uncle Quay, Uncle Murray and Uncle Bob Swisher, would come from where they lived near Pittsburgh, Pennsylvania to hunt with them.

One time when my father and my Uncle Arthur Harriger (Dad's brother-in-law) were talking about farming and crops, I was sitting in the room with them. Uncle Arthur said that he had planted corn and it had come up in two days. I smiled, and he must have thought I didn't believe him because whenever Uncle Arthur saw me after that, he would ask me if I remembered that big lie he told. Funny thing is, I know from experience that flowers and vegetables actually can sprout and come through the ground in two days with the right moisture and temperature. For people who love growing things, seeing those new sprouts is very satisfying. I think my father's sister, Lizzie, and Uncle Arthur were jokesters. Aunt Lizzie once told me that she had a package of something and the directions said to "keep under refrigeration" but since she didn't have a refrigerator, she put it under the cupboard. I hope it was a joke.

I remember an exhilarating feeling in the spring when there would be very strong winds. We would go to the top of a very steep hill and run down with the wind almost holding us back. Most city children have never experienced that.

Every spring we ate a lot of dandelions with hot bacon dressing. My mother would go out and put quite a bit of time into cutting dandelions because it took a huge pan full for a meal. We always had them with boiled potatoes.

Mother dried fruit and that allowed us to have pies made from dried apples in the winter, which was a wonderful treat. She also dried green beans and made her own lard from pig fat. She would cook and make a healing salve from the sticky buds that fell from what we called our bambaguila tree.

Homemade ice cream made with our own strawberries and peaches was a real summer treat because we didn't get it very often. We already had the cream, eggs and strawberries so my father only had to borrow an ice cream maker. It took a lot of cranking, and I remember it took ice and salt. We would get impatient waiting for it to be done. I don't know why it is, but homemade ice cream seems colder than commercial ice cream.

We had an electric cream separator on the farm that was amazing to watch. You pour the whole milk into a large container on top of this machine with two spouts, one for cream and one for skimmed milk. We put a crock under the one for cream and a milk pail for the skimmed milk. We saved enough whole milk for our own use and separated the rest. We gave the skimmed milk to the pigs. They loved it.

If we hadn't made our own, Ruth and I would walk to the Trading Post on Sundays to buy ice cream. We would buy a pint each and eat it with the wooden spoon that they gave us. Trading post ice cream was commercial, but it was very likely made from the cream from our cows since my father sold cream to the ice cream plant in Punxsutawney.

Ruth and I and our neighbors, Clara Jane and Thelma Bargerstock often walked 3 miles to Punxsutawney on

Saturday evenings where we would buy ice cream cones and walk around town eating them. We often went to the movies, too, and if our friends didn't have the money to see one, we would pay their way because we had our money that we had earned working in the gardens. I can't remember for sure now, but the movie was either five cents or ten.

When Ruth and I went to the movies we liked adventure and suspense, but most of all we liked romance stories. Ruth especially liked Richard Widmark. She said he had the bluest eyes. After one movie that I saw with Douglas Fairbanks Jr. in it, I was painfully in love with him. We liked such actors as Clark Gable, Robert Taylor, Henry Fonda, Errol Flynn, Gary Cooper, John Wayne, Tyrone Power, James Cagney, James Stewart, Gregory Peck, Lauren Bacall, Rita Hayworth, Ingrid Bergman, Bette Davis, Loretta Young, Greer Garson and too many more to mention.

We children all went barefoot at home in the summer and even worked in the garden without shoes. We each had a pair of shoes to wear to church or visiting, but as soon as it was warm enough we went without shoes. Of course, when we put the shoes back on in the fall, it was common for them to be tight and uncomfortable until we got used to wearing them again.

Sometimes if we were low on homemade bread I would be sent a mile to Cloe for a loaf of ten cent bread. At times the blacktop roads would be so hot on my bare feet that I could barely take it. Occasionally, I'd take breaks to stand in shaded grass and cool them down.

We always looked forward to spring when we would be allowed to quit wearing our long underwear. They made going to the bathroom hard. I would get upset because I couldn't get my stockings up over the legs of my long underwear without pulling the underwear up also. Try it.

We had a large back yard with thick green grass. My father put lime on it to improve it. We played in the yard a lot. We tumbled, stood on our heads and tried to do cartwheels.

One day my brother Bob was playing with a broom handle. I was sitting on the ground when he decided to swing the handle around and see how close to the top of my head he could get. He hit my nose and it spurted blood. I wasn't angry at him because I knew he felt bad and hadn't meant to hurt me.

There was a huge beech tree just across the road from our home. The beechnuts were small, triangular shaped nuts and were very tasty. We also dug sassafras roots to make tea. There were a lot of birch trees and we liked to chew the bark off the new, tender growth of the branches.

In late summer when the grain crops had to be harvested, Dad would hire some young men from Cloe to help. I think they would have worked just for the meals. Mom made a big cooked meal at noon and again at 5:30.

In 1936 when I was 9, a terrible flood hit Punxsutawney and it rained and rained for days. The little creek beside out home became a surging river. The water rose and rose until it flooded our basement. We were all worried because the Cloe Dam was directly above our home. If the breast of the dam had broken, we all would have been washed away.

We seldom went to the doctor. We used home remedies and they worked just fine. We all survived. But every now and again something would happen and we would actually need a doctor. When I was around 10, my mother had a ruptured appendix. She was very sick – near dying. The doctor who treated her gave up and said there was nothing more he could do for her. We were all very worried. June and Kay took over all the cooking and laundry and the rest of us all pitched in wherever we could. My father wasn't a quitter like that old doctor, though, and he found a young doctor who had a new method of draining poison. That doctor saved her life. I think penicillin was new then, but I don't know if my mother was given any at that time by that wonderful young doctor.

In the spring my father would tap maple trees for maple sap. They would boil the sap in a large iron kettle over a fire to make maple syrup. They also made apple butter in this large kettle in the fall.

Aunt Irene would visit in the summer and she always brought a large container of her orange cookies. I still have the recipe and have made them nearly every year at Christmastime.

There were times in late summer when the watermelon and cantaloupe were all ripe at once. We would set up a table in the back yard and invite relatives to come and enjoy them with us. The official family reunions were held at Grandfather Frederick's until most of the family was grown up. They set everyone up at a huge table on the main floor in the barn.

Chapter 6 - Animals

Very exciting things can happen on a farm, especially when animals are involved. One summer day in 1939 when I was 12, two cows got out of the pasture and ran off. They ran through the fields and past homes all the way to Cloe, a full mile away. My brother Floyd and I ran after them and finally caught up with them. It was really difficult because we had no way to get hold of them, but we were able to steer them in the right direction and chase them back home.

We had a couple of different dogs over the years, but the most adorable one was Nipper. Whenever a picture was being taken, he'd show up and make sure he was in it. We had cats in the barn to catch mice, but we never had pets in the house until most of us were grown and moved out. Then Dad got a beautiful little black Pomeranian named Cubby. Cubby got out one day, went on the road and was hit by a car. After a couple of years Dad got a light-colored Pomeranian named Wiggy.

Our landlord Mr. Brown once gave us an old mule named Nellie. Dad built us a wooden cart that we hooked to her and she would pull it to give us rides -- if she felt like it. Nellie definitely lived up to the reputation of mules being stubborn. She often refused to budge even an inch until she was good and ready.

It was always a sad occasion when a farm animal would die, especially a horse. My father would call Mr. Katz to remove them and he would take the horses to a factory where they made dog food or fertilizer.

It was exciting when there was a calf or a litter of pigs born. One of my favorite chores was to go to the chicken coop to gather the eggs.

I always had the attitude that I could do most anything, so when Mother once said that she wanted a chicken to cook, I said, "I can kill one."

Knowing I had never done it, she looked at me and asked, "Can you?"

There was a wooden chopping block beside the shed and an axe inside it. I went to the coop, caught a chicken and pulled its wings down to its feet. I held the feet and wings in my left hand, laid its head down on the chopping block and chopped with the axe. I quickly grabbed the neck so it wouldn't flop and spray blood on me. I did everything right my very first time, but my mother just watched and didn't say a word. That was my mother – a person of few words.

I was very anxious to be allowed to milk a cow. As soon as I was big enough to carry a large pail of milk, I eagerly took on the responsibility of milking one cow each morning and evening. I was probably 10 years old and continued until I was 14 and starting high school. My younger brothers were big enough by then to take over.

My father and older brothers butchered cows and pigs. We had the best meat there was. Part of our shed was a smokehouse where we cured sausage, hams and bacon.

Chapter 7 - The Farmers Market

My father grew all kinds of vegetables that he sold at the Farmers market. The market was held in a designated area in the public square in downtown Punxsutawney every Saturday morning. After a number of years, he heard about a market in DuBois, Pennsylvania held on Friday evenings. He joined the market and helped form an association that, among other things, built a building to hold the market in.

Dad did well at the markets. Besides the vegetables, he took fresh, cleaned chickens and flowers. We kids all had our chances to help at the market and sometimes my mother would go. Killing and cleaning chickens became a Friday chore that I was not fond of. It took three or four of us to get them all done.

Once the market members decided to put on a show. My sisters Kay, June and I sang the song, "Whispering Hope." I was 11 years old and I really did whisper, being too shy to sing very loud.

Chapter 8 - Taking Responsibility

I always saved money and when I bought something or spent some, I never spent it all. When I was 14, I took some money I had saved and walked three miles to the dentist in Punxsutawney to get two small cavities in my front teeth fixed. I've always been thankful that I did that. The same teeth have been refilled three times and I still have them at age 90.

When I was 11 years old, I ordered a Brownie Ansco camera and a tiny blue bottle of Evening in Paris perfume from the Sears Roebuck catalog. I felt very proud because I bought it with the money I had earned working in the garden. I have been taking pictures ever since.

I always saved money for the summer celebration in the town square of Punxsutawney. I loved riding the fastest rides I could find and the Ferris wheel.

My father entered me in the 4-H club one year. I was to raise capons from chick to market. I fed and watered them faithfully until it was time for the judging. The entry had to be a dressed capon cleaned and dressed for market. It was to be judged by size, weight and appearance and I had to keep a record of what kind and how much food they ate daily. My father picked the one he thought was best and we killed and cleaned it. My father came with me to the judging and banquet and I felt like Queen for a Day. My capon won third prize, but I was told that if my record keeping had been better, I would have won first prize. That was a lesson to remember. I have to laugh at that poor, naked capon being called dressed, though, because it was actually the most undressed it had ever been.

My father obviously knew that the way to get the most work out of his kids was to do it alongside them. When there was planting, weeding or picking to be done, he'd call out, "Come on, kids. Let's go!"

Dad had a set rate he paid us for picking produce. He paid one cent a quart for strawberries, one cent a pound for beans and peas. There were nine pounds in a peck. If there was nothing to be picked he would give us a small allowance each week. We learned to appreciate hard work and it helped us learn to manage money. Once Ruth and I were paid ten cents a row for weeding beets and carrots. Because of the grade in the field, we couldn't even see the end of the rows when we started.

I enjoyed polishing shoes. For several years when I was maybe 11 to 13, I would polish my brothers' and parents' shoes. My brother Lee had a pair of brown and white shoes he wore in the summer that were difficult to polish, and Lee knew it, so a couple of times he gave me 10 cents.

Sarah Swisher (Mother) 22 years old

Frank Frederick (Father) 24 years old

The farm, our homestead

Grandparents on Frederick (Dad's) Side of Family

Aunt Lizzie (Dad's sister) and Uncle Arthur

Frederick Children

Frederick Children – Ruth, Mary, Jim, Bob, Richie - 1939

Bell School grades 1 through 8

Me and Teddy in front of our farmhouse

Mary, Jim, Nipper the wonder dog, Richard; 1940

Jim in band uniform, Dick, and Nipper who got into
every picture he could, uninvited

Ruth, 13, and Mary, 11; Mom in window; 1938

Jim, 16 years old

Mom and the girls on the bridge next to the farm
in 1942

Dad and my brothers before Lee left for WW II

Me, Helen, Kay, Bob, Jim, baby Billy Blair in the
front yard under the bambaguilia tree

Me, 16 years old, 1944; on the bridge I hand-walked
under when I was 11

Mary Frederick (me) 1945 Graduation PHS

Me with friends Clara Jane and Betty Jane, 1944

Kay (my sister) and Wilson Blair

Violet, Wanda and Floyd (my brother) Frederick

Glenn and Ruth (my sister) Smith

Helen and Lee (my brother) Frederick

Bob (my brother) and Norma Frederick

Bob at graduation

Larry, my sister June, Fred, me and Terry in 1952

Terry and Bill Blair, 1952

My brother Dick, LaRue, and little Richie

My sister Hazel, Joe, Terry and Fred in 1954

My husband Fred who fought in WW II

Fred the hunter

Terry, Bill, me and Fred in 1965

Terry in 5th grade

Bill, 3 years old

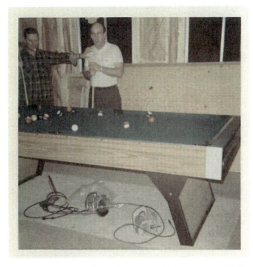

My husband Fred and Wayne Dicks

Me tree climbing in 1985 and 1971

Jay and Mary Dickman wedding

Me at Skypark with our Cessna

My awards for spot landing and bomb drop in 1983

Jay and me at Skypark in front of our Cessna
Skylane 182 RG in 1987

Plane Janes in 1987

Meg Reitz, Norma McWherter and me on a trip

Skypark Airport 1976

My parents in their 60's, Frank and Sarah Frederick

Me at work

At my retirement from Parker Hannifin Corp. in 1991

Parker Hannifin Corporation
Gas Turbine Fuel Systems Division
184 Columbia Street
Clyde, NY 14433 USA
Phone (315) 923-2911

May 9, 1989

To Whom It May Concern:

My association with Mary Dickman enveloped 6 years at Parker Hannifin. During this time, she worked under my supervision either directly or indirectly in our Assembly and Test Department. In our prototype environment Mary developed many technical skills, an understanding of fluid control and the mechanics of assembly work.

Mary has always been a reliable, mature employee. The nature of our business demanded response at a moments notice and Mary always put in the effort and overtime without complaint. Pressure never phased Mary and she maintained her pleasant personality throughout.

I highly recommend Mary Dickman for employment in any company that desires an employee who adapts well in every environment, old fashioned hard work and total dedication to company goals.

Sincerely,

Michael Roth
Plant Manager

62

June's neighbors, Mr. & Mrs. Bill Brumfield's cow
that we snuck into their yard

Reunion at my niece Gail's cabin in 2001

Babysitting Alison

April, Terry's daughter, age 14

My Grandsons, Shawn and Jason and my son Terry

Taylor Seaton with Great Great Grandson Uriah, his birthday
is the same as mine, September 16th

Me at German Christmas Party

My snowblower that I altered with a coffee can

My dear friend Kathy and me in Chicago

Me playing Scrabble with Kathy

Bill, Pamela, and Alison Potts and Brooke Belvin

Alison and Kanen Coffey

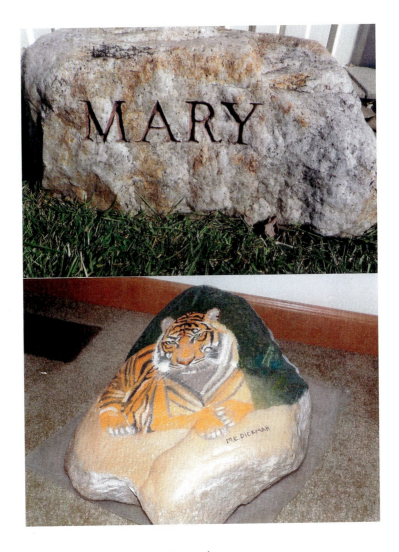

My rocks

Me with my paintings at the German Club

Me with my paintings in 2005

Me wearing my Ivanka Trump dress at 90

Gobblers Knob in 2017

Nieces Mary Linda and Cheryl in 2017 on bridge that
WPA built

Chapter 9 - Things I Shouldn't Have Done

When I was in seventh grade I bought Bugler tobacco and rolled my own cigarettes. There was a very big sewer pipe under the road that was big enough to stand in, so that's where my friend Ed Wachob and I would go to smoke.

I'm sure my mother must have smelled the smoke on me, but she never said anything. Just another time I remember when she had no comment. I imagine she thought things would resolve themselves and she was right. When the Wachobs moved away, I quit smoking.

On the road between home and school there was a railroad tracks and a large metal bridge over a sulfur creek. Railcars would be stopped there and we would walk along the tracks, not knowing when the cars would start moving. One time my friend Ed got in one of the cars because he saw it had bananas in it.

I would climb up on the bridge and I also "hand-walked" the underside of the bridge across the creek. I could do that then – my arms were strong from milking the cows, cleaning and working in the garden.

The State Highway trucks carried heavy loads so they couldn't get up the hill very fast and there were often chains hanging from the tailgate. Once on my way home from school when a truck was moving slowly, I took hold of the chain and ran behind the truck until it got going too fast for me to keep up. I'm not sure why I did this. It must have felt like a challenge to me, but this stunt was probably my most dangerous.

Chapter 10 - Lee's Accident 1946

My brother Lee and his wife Helen had just gotten married. They were living at home on the farm while Helen worked in a Punxsutawney beauty shop as a hairdresser. I was 19 and still at home, as was my brother Bob who was 17. It would be another year before he left to join the Air Force.

Lee and Bob were repairing the barn roof when Lee fell off the roof. My Grandfather Frederick was on a chair in the backyard watching. He thought it was Bob who fell because Bob hadn't been wearing the right kind of shoes for the work he was doing.

I called Helen at work to tell her what happened. Mother and I walked out to the barn when the ambulance came and took Lee to the Punxsutawney hospital. He had a broken elbow and a broken thigh bone. The doctor put a plate in his leg and it got infected. They finally took him to DuBois Hospital where he had another surgery with a different doctor. It took him a very long time to heal.

Chapter 11 - Sports

I always loved participating in sports. In grade school we had athletic meets with other schools. I participated in high jump, foot races, pole vault and relay races.

In high school I played softball, basketball, hockey and relay races. I won my letter in High School Athletics.

The strange part about my participation in sports is that not one person in my family ever saw me compete. Two girls' teams played basketball at the halftime of our school's competition against another high school. From a long distance I made a one-handed basket and was able, once again, to claim the title of Queen for the Day. That evening the people in the bleachers stood up and cheered. I just wish my family could have seen me do it.

When I played softball after school I had no ride so had to walk home three miles.

Chapter 12 - Minor Accidents

One evening in 1942 the weather was snowy and freezing and I was going to ride into town with my friends. The older cars had running boards along the sides and when I stepped up on it, my foot slipped off. My leg hit the running board hard and my shinbone got chipped. My leg was very sore and swollen for weeks and the soreness in one spot remained sensitive for years. Despite the pain, I didn't go to a doctor and I didn't change anything I was doing.

When I was about 24 years old, Fred, Cliff, his girlfriend Virginia and I were riding around Punxsutawney. I was driving. We were looking for a parking spot so we could go into a restaurant. We drove round and round, and finally I saw a diagonal space. I said, "Oh, here's one," and I zipped into it. Soon we realized the reason it was open was because it was too narrow, and we couldn't get either door open. I tried to back out but couldn't because I had bumped into the bumper of the car in front and they were locked. Cliff volunteered to climb out the window and he jumped on the bumper while I backed up, which unlocked it. That was a new experience, not to be repeated.

Chapter 13 - A Dangerous Error

In 1944 when I was 16, my sisters invited me to visit them in Niagara Falls. June and Kay had a room and Hazel and her husband Joe lived there also.

I spent the night with June and Kay and I was supposed to go to Hazel's in the morning. Before she left for work that morning, June told me to go to the corner and catch the #12 bus to Whirlpool Street.

I went to the wrong corner and stood there waiting for the #12 bus. A couple of busses passed by but they weren't the right ones. I was getting very anxious when a nice man stopped and asked me where I wanted to go. He had seen the busses stop and go and saw I was still there. I told him I wanted to go to Whirlpool Street where my sister lived. We didn't talk – he just took me to Whirlpool Street. I don't know what I would have done if he hadn't come along, but it's a different world today when the thought of a young girl walking away with a stranger sends shivers up the spine.

While I was in Niagara Falls my brother-in-law took me for a ride on the Maid of the Mist, a boat on the Niagara River.

My sister June took me shopping and bought me a beautiful dress. The top was black velvet and the skirt was pastel green taffeta with delicate colored stripes.

I want to mention here that it was my brother-in-law Joe Zufall who kept me from quitting high school in my freshman year. I was very discouraged because I had gotten a failing grade in English. My teacher, Mrs. Coleman, was really into classic literature but I just couldn't get interested in it and didn't see the point of it all. Joe gave me a real pep talk that convinced me it was extremely important to finish high school. I have always been grateful that I did.

Chapter 14 - Guns

My father had worked several different jobs before settling on farm life. When he and my mother were first married, he had a job as a security guard or policeman, I'm not sure which. He also worked as a stone mason, on an oil drilling rig and in the lumber business, cutting trees.

Father had a handgun he had used on his security job. It was kept on top of the cupboard in the kitchen along with a couple of pipes which he smoked occasionally. That's also where he usually kept a switch from a tree branch to be used for correction during the rare times when someone misbehaved.

The rifle and shotgun were kept in a gun cabinet in the corner of the pantry next to the sink. The cabinet had no lock; it didn't even have a door, but we kids never touched the guns. We knew they weren't something to play with.

In the year 2000 when Al Gore was running for president, I thought there was a chance he could win. He was advocating gun control and sounded like he didn't believe in the Second Amendment. I decided he wasn't going to take away my right to own a gun, so my friend and I went to the Andover Hardware and I bought a .22-caliber handgun. In 2001 we went to a gun show and I bought a .22 Ruger and a .45 Colt. I went to the shooting range with my next-door neighbor Gus and I came very close to hitting the bullseye.

In December 2017 I went to Point Blank Range with my son Bill, my granddaughter Alison and my grandson Kanen. I was amused when, after seeing my shooting, the manager told me, "I'm glad you're on our side." I saved the target.

Chapter 15 - Berry Picking and Harvesting Time

It was a big event when blackberries and blueberries were ripe. There were large patches of gooseberries, blackberries and blueberries. When I think of picking blueberries, the same memories come to mind. The blueberries were on the top of a very steep hill and on hot days the locusts would sing their loudest. I thought the blueberries were beautiful.

There would be at least five or six of us going picking at one time. The blackberries were on a slanted hillside with thick growth. It was exciting and a true challenge to entirely fill a pail with berries.

When we got home, we would go through the berries and wash them. Mother canned them and usually made some jam. Picking the berries as they ripened and preserving them was an ongoing task each summer.

Planting and harvesting potatoes is very different from growing other vegetables. If you notice, in the spring of the year when you have kept potatoes a little too long, they will grow sprouts in several places and these can be used as seed potatoes. You can cut them in two or three pieces and plant them, they will grow as long as they have a sprout. To plant fields of potatoes, we would plow long furrows to make rows. We would tie a binder twine rope to the front corner of a burlap bag and tie it to the back corner also. Fill the bag with seed potatoes, put it over your shoulder and drop them in the row. Then cover them with soil using your foot.

To dig them is different, also. We would plow a furrow next to the plants to expose the potatoes. Of course, you have to dig a little to uncover some of them. This takes a lot of bending and picking. They can't be pulled out of the ground by the tops like carrots, beets and onions. Potatoes are one of my favorites.

Chapter 16 - Holidays and Birthdays

When I was growing up in a family of ten, birthdays were not celebrated. There were three of us who had June birthdays but June was a very busy month on the farm so there were no celebrations. Money was another issue – there simply wasn't any with which to buy gifts.

We moved to the farm during the depression and for the first few years, there was no money for Christmas presents or birthday parties, cakes and gifts. At Christmas the older children would go into the woods and cut down a tree. We made decorations out of paper, made paper chains for it, and strung popcorn. I remember one year we hung up our stockings and we each got an orange and some candy.

Our Church would give us each a small box of candy for Christmas, an assortment with a little bit of hard candy, chocolate drops and chocolate with nuts or caramel. I tried to trade off with my siblings because I didn't like the chocolate drops with just cream centers.

One year I had been looking at the Sears Catalogue so much that I almost had the doll page worn out. I can't remember how old I was the Christmas I got a doll, but I was so overjoyed that I had tears in my eyes. That same year my brother Bob got a toy car. When you pushed down on it and let it go, it would race across the floor. He was as excited about his gift as I was about mine.

We always had good food and could have ham, roast beef or chicken for Christmas dinner. Mother would bake raisin filled cookies, mince meat pies, and custard fruit pies from canned peaches or berries.

We never had turkey on Thanksgiving because we didn't raise them, so mostly had ham, stuffed roasted chicken, or roast beef. But chicken was not my father's favorite meat. He preferred pork loin roast, roast beef or baked ham. Mother baked pumpkin pies, and our side dishes were mashed potatoes, gravy, cole slaw and canned peas, beans or corn.

When we were older, as many as could would come home for Thanksgiving and Christmas. Once there were grandchildren, it became too much to buy gifts for everyone, so Mother suggested drawing names. We did that for a few years, and it worked out fine.

After we moved to the farm in Punxsutawney, my parents only went to church a few times. We children attended Sunday School and I was baptized when I was 10 years old and given a Bible by a man who donated Bibles to the Church. That would have made Bob 8, Dick 6 and Jim 4 at that time.

At Easter time we always thought people were supposed to have a new outfit, so Mother made new dresses for the girls and shirts for the boys. When the girls got older we made our own dresses. Ladies wore hats then and at Easter they called them Easter bonnets. When I was older I had hats with veils, with wide brims and two pillbox styles like Jackie Kennedy wore. About 6 years ago, I gave some of my old hats to my friend Kathy's granddaughters to play dress up.

Halloween was fun at the farm. We had lots of pumpkins to make jack-o-lanterns. We also had ripe field corn to shell for throwing at peoples' windows. The corn crib was full of corn to grind into food for the chickens, pigs and cows. We had wheat, oats and barley ground in with the corn. I'm afraid we did soap some windows, which wasn't a nice thing to do. At school we had Halloween costume day and the teacher would try to guess who we were. We didn't buy costumes, we just wore clothes that were too big with paper masks and hats.

Valentine's Day was fun at school. The first few years we made paper valentines at home, but in later years we were able to buy some. You could get a whole bag of them for a few cents. There was usually someone" special" who you would give the nicest one to.

I hear people say how birthdays are not the same when they get older, but mine have just kept getting better. In 1997 when I was 69, my daughter-in-law Pam surprised me by having pink elephants put in my yard. I was hoping the neighbors wouldn't think I had the problem of drinking so much that I was seeing pink elephants. When Pam was fifty, I reciprocated and had pink elephants put in her yard so her neighbors could wonder about her.

In 2008 on my 80th birthday, my wonderful neighbors on Havenhurst Court, Bellflower Terrace Condos had a birthday party for me at the Branding Iron Restaurant in Mentor, Ohio. The restaurant had a wooden horse that the birthday person had to sit on and have their picture taken wearing a cowboy hat. We all had a great time.

Chapter 17 - Fred Potts

I met Fred Potts in 1946 through a mutual friend. He was home on leave from the Navy. We dated and when he returned to base, we wrote to each other. Fred came from a family of eight. He had four sisters and three brothers. His mother died when he was 7 years old. His father had several different housekeepers through the years.

When Fred was 12, his father married Margaret Wulfert, whose 14-year-old son Clifford became Fred's stepbrother. When Fred was 16, he lied about his age and joined the Navy.

I was working at Sylvania when Fred was discharged from the Navy in July, 1948, and like a couple of dumb kids, we eloped to Baltimore, Maryland and were married.

Fred had no car, no job and very little money. I was sharing an apartment with two other women and it wouldn't have worked out for us to live there, so Fred's stepmother asked us to live with her temporarily. We visited my parents regularly.

Fred got a job on the railroad, which he didn't like very much. We rented a four-room duplex at 105 Clark Terrace in Punxsutawney and bought furniture on payments. I got a job working days at a factory that made small electrical parts for radios.

One day I bought an ironing board and carried it about a quarter of a mile home. It's amazing what people can do when they set their minds to something. I would walk three miles to my parents' house to wash our clothes – I had never heard of a laundromat. Sometime later I was able to buy a washing machine. Not being familiar with it, I put a load of clothes in and let them wash without realizing that when the cycle was through, it would pump the water out. I hadn't put the hose in the sink and water went all over the kitchen floor. Life was not easy, but it was interesting and we weren't used to having things easy, anyway.

My first pregnancy was normal but our son arrived six weeks early at 4 pounds, 2 ounces. My cousin Ruth Spence came from Clairton, Pennsylvania and stayed a week to help me. Terry was born June 24, 1949 and when he was 3 months old we moved to Youngstown, Ohio where Fred had gotten a job in a steel mill. Our friends Dick and Irene Rearick and Fred's stepbrother Cliff Wulfert and his wife Virginia also lived in Youngstown.

We moved into a three room, first floor apartment at 609 Elm Street. We had a bathroom and basement privileges for doing laundry. The landlord and his wife were always anxious to babysit for us so I could go shopping and we could go out with our friends.

We lived in that apartment for 3 years, and in that time, we bought our first black and white television. One winter while we lived there, we had such deep snow that all the streets were closed. Fred walked to work that day.

There was a small cottage advertised for much less rent, so we moved to 813 ½ Woodland. The owners of the cottage also owned the home in front of it and they lived upstairs. The cottage was heated by a small gas heater. One cold night the heater quit working and I tried to light it. When it ignited, I burned my arm, but it still wasn't lit. I had to call the landlord. I'm sure he smelled the Vicks VapoRub I put on my burnt arm, but he didn't say anything.

When Terry was 4, I suffered through a miscarriage. When he was 5, I put him in kindergarten, but he wasn't going very long when the school contacted me and said he caught ringworm on his head from some of the other students. I took him to the doctor and he prescribed some medication and told me to buy an ultraviolet bulb. In a dark closet the ringworm would glow under the ultraviolet light and I would scrub at them with a toothbrush. I decided not to send Terry back to school and taught him at home.

When Terry was small, between 1951 and 1955, Fred's sister Minnie and her husband and children lived near us. We spent a lot of time together and I remember going on picnics with them in the summer.

Our next move was to a six-room house at 619 Lexington Ave. It had a basement, kitchen and bath. We lived in the Lexington Ave. house for 3 1/2 years and made a number of improvements while there. Bill was born in 1957 while we lived in that large house. We rented a bedroom to a young woman named Rosemary Michele who had been living next door to our small cottage home. She ate her meals with us and she loved helping with baby Bill. She was like part of our family, but sadly, she passed away from stomach cancer shortly after she was married, at the age of 30.

Besides working his job at the steel mill, Fred had a part time job helping Wayne Dicks install television antennas on roofs. We were friends with Wayne and Eleanor Dicks and played cards with them occasionally. I got excited when Wayne told us about a development of new homes in Weathersfield Township because I had been saving up to make a down payment on a house.

We went and looked at the model homes and ordered a three-bedroom ranch house to be built at 60 Chestnut Street. This was a very exciting move to go into a brand-new home where we had chosen the colors of the floor tiles, woodwork and walls. I made all the drapes and curtains so it really felt like ours.

The neighbors were all young people with school aged children and we quickly became friends with most of them. The people on one side of us were good people but didn't talk much to anyone. We became friends with George and Janet Raidel and we played cards with them sometimes. We went out to the saloons regularly with three other couples. Fred and I spent New Year's Eve with friends. We usually went out to where there was music and dancing. A few times there were house parties.

Terry had a nice social life, too. He walked to school with several friends and joined the Boy Scouts with the neighbor boys. Billy was just a baby, only 10 months old, when we moved in.

We invited Fred's stepbrother Cliff and his wife Marie to dinner often, but it was never reciprocated. Then Marie confessed to me that she wasn't a very good cook.

Since I didn't work outside my home in my thirties and early forties, I had a lot of time to spend with music. I loved playing stereo albums of my favorites and I still have a stack of them like Floyd Cramer on piano, Lenny Dee on organ, Liberace on piano and by singers like Andy Williams, Eddy Arnold, Elvis Presley, Don Williams, Willy Nelson, Tom Jones, Ray Price and too many more to try to mention them all.

Fred's job at the Steel Mill allowed a lot of idle time so he would take paperback books in his lunch pail nearly every day. He liked western stories, some mysteries and, I suppose, some love stories. He ran what was called a peeler machine that made seamless steel pipes.

Fred always worked for one week on the daytime shift, one week second shift and then one-week night shift. Then he would be off from Friday morning until Tuesday morning. We always enjoyed visiting Punxsutawney if we could get away for the weekend.

When the boys were young, Fred liked to go to drive-in movies and, of course, the snacks were as big a deal as the movie for the boys.

Two or three times a year we spent weekends in Silver Creek, New York with my sister Ruth and her husband Glenn Smith. Sometimes they came to our house, too. On our way to New York, we would stop off at a small restaurant in N. Kingsville where we would get their deep-fried mushrooms. Neither Fred nor I had ever eaten them before but liked them so much that we always stopped for some.

Once when we were on our way to Silver Creek late in the evening we hit two deer. One went over the roof and the other hit the grill and fender. Luckily, Fred was able to maintain control of the car, but the fender cut the tire and the car was disabled. Finally, a good-hearted passerby stopped and we asked him to call my sister for us.

Fred loved hunting and he would hunt in both New York and Pennsylvania. He also loved camping so we went camping when he was on vacation and on some long weekends. We first started camping in a tent and then we bought a pull-along popup camper that was much more comfortable.

I insisted that Fred ask the blessing at mealtimes. We had Terry and Bill baptized and we began attending church. Fred seldom went because of his swing shift job. Terry liked going to church and Bill was alright with it until he got older. Then he'd put up a fight because he didn't like getting dressed up. Bill is 60 now and to this day, he still doesn't like getting dressed up.

In 1960 Fred shot a large wild turkey. I stuffed and roasted the bird and invited some neighbors to eat with us. When I prepare dry bread, I cut it in squares. Richard Coe turned to his wife and said, "Why don't you do that, Edie?" Well, the look she gave him was so scorching I expected him to wilt down to a pile on the floor. I thought it was funny but nobody made a comment of any kind.

In 1964 Fred bought a pool table and had it delivered to our house. I didn't think it was a good idea to turn our living room into a pool hall so we contracted a builder to put on an addition. We wound up having a 20' by 40' room added on the back of the house to accommodate the pool table and got many hours of enjoyment from it.

I have always had a strong drive to do things. When something needs to be done, I want to get it done. When something needs to be repaired, I will find a way. I have never liked the feeling of being dependent on anyone, but that is how Fred wanted it. Fred was always against my getting a job, but after Terry joined the Navy I got a part time job at a ladies' dress shop. The shop closed six months later, so I got a full-time job at a plant that packaged plumbing parts.

Fred and I were married 23 years. Without going into personal details, I'll just say that there are millions of families who are viewed as ideal families. Discontent and grievances don't show. We had a bitter divorce. Fred remarried and I remarried, but within a year, Fred died of a massive heart attack. His new wife got his life insurance and pension. They were expecting a baby girl.

Chapter 18 - Terry

When Terry was 12 and in the Boy Scouts, they went on a camping trip for a week. We expected him to be working hard on earning merit badges, but as it turned out, I think he was homesick, because he spent a lot of time making gifts for me.

We bought a guitar for Terry and he was taking lessons. One day he and his friends were working on a car with it up on jacks. The jack slipped and the car came down and broke Terry's arm. That was the end of the guitar lessons.

Terry was very ambitious. He had a paper route for a couple of years and then he bussed tables at a nice restaurant. After high school, he went to electronics school for a year before joining the Navy. After 4 years in the Navy, he came back home and married Nancy Esenwein. They had three children: April, Shawn and Jason.

Terry and Nancy lived in Girard a while and then moved on to live in several different places, mostly a long distance from me and Jay, like Minnesota and Kentucky. We didn't get to see them as often as we would have liked to so we didn't spend much time together, but we did go to their children's' high school graduations.

Chapter 19 - Bill

Bill was a teaser, even as a boy and he would pick at me until I had enough and would run after him with a wooden spoon. A few times he got a swat on the butt with that famous wooden spoon. I think some of the young ones today could benefit from the use of a paddle of some sort to keep them in line.

After Fred passed away, Bill didn't want to leave his friends in Girard so he lived with Terry and Nancy while he finished school. After high school he went to machinists' school and then came to Cleveland and got a job in a machine shop. The equipment was old and he didn't like it so he quit and took a job at the Aeroll Engineering Company.

Bill lived with Jay and me for a few months and then got an apartment. He moved a couple of times, between Girard and Cleveland, and then bought a mobile home in Madison. He reconnected with an old girlfriend from high school who had a 4-year-old daughter from a previous marriage. Bill and Pamela Tascione were married and they lived in his mobile home for 2 years. Together they had a baby girl, Alison, before buying a home with four and a half acres in Geneva. Pamela worked as a paralegal for attorneys.

Chapter 20 - My Love of Music

I always loved music and wanted to learn to play an instrument. When I was 26, I bought a little concertina. I played around with it but never quite mastered it.

We were never taught music in school, but I had a friend who could read music and showed me which notes were on which lines. I started practicing and wrote notes on staff paper. It was then I bought a Frontalini chord organ and practiced until I could play a number of songs. Then I bought an electronic organ called an Electrovoice and practiced more. Because I wanted a better organ sound, I bought a Hammond organ.

On a little cassette player, I recorded several tapes of me playing my Electro Voice organ, the one I had before I got the Hammond, which would have sounded better. At that time, I knew at least twenty songs without looking at the music. It was easy for me to find time to practice because Fred worked different shifts and when he worked 3 to 11 p.m., I could play all evening. I have to confess, I don't know those songs anymore, having been away from them for so many years. I knew them by heart back then but would have to look at the music to play them now.

Here are some of my favorite songs that I knew by heart and used to play all the time. "Love is Blue," "Please Release Me," "PS I Love You," "Spanish Eyes," "There Goes my Everything," "Make the World Go Away," "I'll Never Fall in Love Again," "I Can't Help Falling in Love with You," "Quentin's Theme, " "Perfidia," and "Green Sleeves."

Terry's friend Bill Modarelli was an accomplished organist and he played for us quite often. When Billy was 7, he began playing by ear. I thought he had talent that should be developed so I had him take lessons. He did well, but he was a kid so it was hard to get him to sit still long enough to practice. He was ready for a recital, but, instead, I gave in and let him quit. Bill was born with some real musical talent, perhaps he could have become as successful as the virtuoso organist Lenny Dee.

Chapter 21 - Jay Dickman

I'm not sure why I was attracted to my second husband, Jay Dickman. He was tall like my father but he didn't talk very much.

Jay and his first wife had no children. He had two sisters, Jane and Marion. Marion had a son who was married and had a son of his own. Jane was married but had no children. Jay's family had lived in Cleveland before they moved to Binghamton, New York. Jay's sister Marion lived in Fort Worth, Texas. She came to visit us in 1985 while she checked on some businesses in Cleveland, and we took her around Cleveland to see the changes in the area where they had lived. Jay's sister Jane lived in Pomona, New York and visited in 1982. We took her for an airplane ride to New Philadelphia for dinner where we often went for Sunday breakfast. Jane came to visit us again in 1993 when Jay was bedfast, just before he passed away.

Jay never told me he wanted to be a pilot, but when we were dating he took me to the Youngstown Airport and paid for me to go up in a plane with an instructor. It was my first flying lesson.

He would take me to the restaurant at Burke Lakefront Airport and we would sit by the windows so we could see the airplanes take off and land. Jay had already soloed in an airplane but becoming a pilot had never been on my "to-do" list.

Jay and I were married in Euclid, Ohio in the Lake Shore Methodist Church. Our attendants were Edwin and Alta Woodard. We went on a long driving trip to New Jersey, New York and Pennsylvania after the wedding so he could meet some of my brothers and sisters. Then he took me to Alliance, Ohio to meet the Gotts, the couple he had lived with as a boy.

Syd and Doris Gott were good people. They had four daughters and one son and they obviously liked moving. They had lived in Pennsylvania, New York, Texas, Vermont and went several times back to Ohio where their children lived.

We rented a second-floor apartment and lived at 328 Goller Ave. for two years. During the summer a young man who lived on our street was speeding and ran into my car as I was turning into my driveway. I wasn't hurt but my car was badly damaged.

Jay was working at a rubber manufacturing company and I got a job at Parker Hannifin across the street from Jay's job. I liked my job. It was in research and development of jet fuel nozzles.

We saved a little money and then borrowed enough for a down payment on a house in Euclid, Ohio at 2114 Algonquin Road in Indian Hills Estates. It was a brick ranch with a full basement and a double garage. There was a large back yard where, after a few years, I put in a vegetable garden. I had forgotten how much I loved to grow things. The garden was mine to work – Jay didn't work in it and he didn't shovel snow. We had a regular power lawn mower which I used and I bought a small snow blower which I used along with a very good snow shovel. Jay bought a large tractor riding mower and a huge snow plow which had to be mounted on it, but he never put it on.

When I had been working at Parker Hannifin fifteen years, I was offered the position of supervisor in the Jets division of the Parker branch which was located in Clyde, New York. I didn't accept it because I am a hands-on worker, not a supervisor. Besides, I didn't want to move, nor did my husband Jay, so we stayed in Euclid.

Jay heard about a ground school class for pilot licenses in Cleveland. He enrolled us and we attended for 6 weeks, but we weren't satisfied at how we were learning so we quit.

Jay saw an airplane advertised in the paper that was in a hangar in Wadsworth, Ohio. We went there to look at it and bought it. They were having ground school at Skypark Airport so we enrolled, finished, took the test, and we both passed. This was 1975.

Learning to fly was a challenge for me, but I never doubted that I could do it. I was working a lot of overtime on my job and I had to drive an hour each way to take flying lessons in Wadsworth. As each step of the training was accomplished, I was closer to becoming a pilot. It was most exciting when I was up there flying all by myself. Virginia Hanic was my main flight instructor, but over the years for my annual flight review, I flew with many other instructors. Ruby Menching gave me the flight test. She had quite a history because she had flown B1 Bombers over the ocean in World War II.

Jay completed his flying lessons and passed the test. I waited for Jay to get his license and then I started flying. I waited for him to get his license first, because it would not have been good if I passed and he didn't. Flying had always been his dream – not mine. I received my pilot's license in November, 1975 just before we went for a 10-day vacation trip with a large group of friends from Skypark Airport. As many as eight to twelve airplanes would go on vacation and holiday trips and we made reservations ahead of time for the motels and restaurants.

In 1977, Jay and I went to Instrument Training Class at Wadsworth and we both passed the written test. Jay started the instrument flying and got his rating. I didn't go for the rating because it was intensive training and was too much added in with all the overtime I was working. I was still able to go on trips with just my private license, so that was good enough for me.

Over the course of 25 years of going on trips, we have been in most of the states and went to the Bahamas twice. We had a lot of excitement and our share of both good and bad experiences. The men in the flying club would go on weekend trips in March and the women would go on their own trip in April each year. On other holidays and the fall vacations, we all went together.

Once Jay came home from Florida in freezing rain and made a very hard landing which ruined our plane's propeller and engine. That year I couldn't use our plane so I went with another lady.

Each year in July, there was a flying contest at Skypark Airport. In 1982, Jay won the spot landing contest and in 1983 I won the spot landing contest. For the flying contest there was a circle on the runway with a line through the middle. The object was to land with the main wheels as close to the line as possible. We were allowed to make two landings. My first landing was only 5' from the line. My second was 20'. The average was 12 ½'. A friend of ours rode along with me just for fun that day. He had planned to enter the contest, too, but after I won with such a small distance, he chose not to fly. Again, I was Queen for a Day. On one of the holiday vacation trips, Dr. Reed who flew at Skypark Airport, said to me, "Do you know you are a legend?"

I had helped keep records for the contest for several years and voluntarily cleaned the airport building many times. At the annual awards dinner in 1982 I was given a silver tray in appreciation.

We took a lot of people for airplane rides. I took one of my foremen and his wife. I also took my union president and his two children, but his little boy got airsick, which ruined his experience. I also took six of my coworkers at different times.

We frequently had parties at the airport where everyone brought a dish of their choice. On Sunday mornings we often flew to New Philadelphia with friends for breakfast.

From 1975-1990 Jay and I spent New Year's Eve at Skypark airport where they had a large party room. It was always a big celebration

I should try to forget about it, but I vividly remember the time Jay bought a new car and didn't take out insurance on it even though I suggested it might be a good idea. When he replied that he was a careful driver, I reminded him that not everyone else was. In one ear and out the other. The first trip we took in that car, we went to see my father in West Virginia and parked on the street in front of his house. When we had been there about an hour and a half, we heard a loud crash. A drunk man with no insurance crashed into Jay's new car and totaled it. $5,000 gone, just like that!

If Jay ever wanted me to do something, he didn't ask – he found a way to force me into it, like that time he insisted I tow his car home, even though I had never done anything like that before. Another time I had to go out with him on a cold winter night when the media was warning people not to go out, and if you did, to be sure you had enough gas. I didn't want to go anywhere that night, but I was obedient, so went along.

Jay hadn't bothered to get gas and, needless to say, we ran out. Jay had trouble with the circulation in his legs and couldn't walk very far without much pain. He had blocked arteries, which also added to his heart problems. Given the circumstances, I was the one who had to walk to a service station and carry a can of gas back to the car. If I hadn't brought my wool hat and mittens along, I would have gotten frostbite. I didn't complain, though. I knew he was good and cold waiting for me in that unheated car.

Jay and I had our differences but things went smoothly most of the time because I would bend to his way of thinking. Revealing the tendency of being controlling, Jay would volunteer me to do favors for friends without asking me if I wanted to do it. He told Art Bishop, a friend and mechanic at Skypark Airport, that I would go after work to Lost Nation Airport and pick up airplane parts at their parts store and bring them to Skypark for him. We lived in Euclid, 50 miles from Euclid to Skypark. I did it once, and we decided it was foolish since Art said he could fly to Lost Nation and get the parts. Of course, after I did that, I could go home and get dinner, and whatever else I needed to do. I guess I just aim to please.

A couple times when we were eating at a Restaurant with friends, Jay popped a surprise on me and said, "This is on Mary." So rather than embarrass everyone, I paid... I think I was too easy going. It seemed easier than bickering to me. I think you could call him a manipulator because he always knew how to get his way.

Over the years Jay worked three different jobs as a maintenance superintendent in the rubber industry. He was working at the last one, which was in Middlefield, Ohio, when he had a heart attack and they let him go. He was 58 years old, had no pension and just a small life insurance policy. After a while Jay got a part time job in Akron. He had more heart problems so had heart bypass surgery in Akron. This made things difficult for me because we lived in Euclid and I worked at Parker Hannifin in Cleveland. During the surgery, the doctor found lymphoma cancer, so Jay went on to receive his treatments in Akron.

Sometime later, our friend Dan Weltzien was diagnosed with cancer of the esophagus and Jay volunteered to take care of Dan's business at the airport where we flew while Dan had surgery and was recuperating. Jay stayed at the airport and I would bring him clean clothes on the weekends. From time to time Jay and I started flying again and we spent nearly every weekend at the airport. We had a room in our hangar with a bed, a heater and a water pan. In the summer I often stayed and spent the nights there with him.

When Jay was unable to work anymore, he started going to a donut coffee shop where he met other retired men. They would buy and trade valuable and collectors coins. I was still working at the time. When I retired in 1991, Jay and I drove to Minnesota to visit Terry and his family.

Jay's legs became worse in 1993. He was bedridden for 6 months before he passed away from heart failure. I decided to stay at my home in Euclid and began babysitting my granddaughter Alison. Bill was working near my home so he would bring her by in the morning and pick her up after work. We did this for two years. Then Pamela's mother moved to Geneva so she could keep Alison. I savor those memories of spending all that wonderful time with my granddaughter Alison.

Chapter 22 - The Plane Janes Trips

The Ladies Club at Skypark Airport in Wadsworth, Ohio was known as The Plane Janes. Some members were pilots and some were married to pilots.

In 1983 I was invited to join The Ninety-Nines, Inc., an international organization of women pilots. I would have loved to be a member, but since I was already a member of The Plane Janes, I simply didn't have time and turned them down.

We Plane Janes had some very exciting trips and always saw interesting things when we arrived at our destinations. At the motels we would gather in one room to visit and have fun.

The first trip I went on was to St. Louis, Missouri. We were confronted by some of the worst weather conditions that occur in April. There was rain and very low clouds. We had to spend an extra night in St. Louis. I remember enjoyable trips to Frankfort, Kentucky; Winston-Salem, North Carolina and Williamsburg, Virginia. On one trip to Gatlinburg, Tennessee we encountered some low clouds.

The trip to Memphis, Tennessee was a nail-biter. We ran into low clouds so I chose to climb up and fly above them. This worked well until it was time to think about landing. We had to fly quite a distance before we found a hole in the clouds that we could go down through.

The Plane Janes trip to West Virginia was one for the books. The wind was so strong that I was unable to land at the airport on our flight plan. It had a north-south runway and the wind was coming straight across it. We had to find an east-west runway so we could land into the wind. It was quite an experience.

On our trip to Louisville, Kentucky we were given some lightning and rain showers. It was unnerving and we were grateful that it didn't last long.

The trip to New Orleans was out of the ordinary. One plane with a pilot and three passengers got off course and didn't make it to our designated airport for gas. We waited there as long as we could but had to leave. We later learned that she had landed at a different airport for gas, but still landed safely at the designated New Orleans airport. When we landed at New Orleans airport it was dark. The flight path to land was over water and the airport is at sea level. Situations like that make you want to kiss the ground.

We ladies had great times on our flying trips. Besides the excitement of flying, we always went some place special where there was something of interest to see. We saw candy factories, pottery plants, glass blowing demonstrations and many more interesting things.

In New Orleans we went for a boat ride on a canal and went to a special show. In St Louis we went up in the famous arches. In Memphis, Tennessee we went to the Fed Ex hub and watched the mail being sorted on large conveyers. Packages were going every which way. In Winston Salem, North Carolina we visited the cigarette factory. In Charleston, South Carolina and Arlington, Virginia we saw many historic homes and shops and in New York we saw the Corning dish factory.

Chapter 23 - Kevin

One evening in 1995 Pamela and I went to a restaurant in Geneva and I met a man who was in real estate. We began spending a lot of time together and he kept me busy until 2005. His parents owned Berkshire Hills Country Club in Chesterland, Ohio and we would go out, pick limbs up off the greens, plant flowers and play a little golf. We also spent time riding around looking for locations for his commercial real estate business.

Once we went to Las Vegas together where he had a meeting with other agents and then we went to see my brother Floyd when he was suffering from bone cancer. We went to Silver Creek, New York to see my sister Ruth. We even went to Punxsutawney for the Groundhogs Day celebrations in 1999. It has become such a popular event that people come from many different states just to be there in the morning when the groundhog does or doesn't see his shadow. It is held on top of a hill just outside of town, and since there isn't enough parking, they have busses available to take people up the hill, starting very early in the morning when it's still dark out. Hundreds of people stand in the cold, and in our case, the snow, with very cold feet. We were fortunate enough to be able to buy hot coffee but both of us agreed that the one time seeing the groundhog was enough.

When Kevin and I were riding around looking for Real Estate sites for businesses, I saw several rocks with people's names on them in their yards. I liked them and I said I would like to have one of those. Several Months later, Kevin surprised me with a beautiful big rock with" Mary" etched on it.

I asked Kevin to help me replace the edging strips around my shrubs where they had come out of the ground. When he was digging he hit into a rock. He kept digging and couldn't believe what he saw. It was a very big rock, and when he cleaned it off, it had a very unusual shape. I said it was too special to throw away, so I did an oil painting of a tiger on it. I have it in my living room. Everyone loves it.

In 2003 when I was 76, Kevin went to my family reunion with me. It was held at the log cabin Lee had built for his daughter Gail, just a short distance from where I grew up. Kevin and I decided to walk over to my old family farmhouse and the lady who was living there was very nice. When I told her I had grown up in her house, she was gracious enough to ask me in to see it. When we were upstairs, I told her how I used to slide downstairs on the banister.

"How did you do that?" She asked.

I said, "Like this." I jumped up on the bannister and I slid all the way down.

The lady's daughter and grandson were downstairs in a back room. They saw me come sliding down and the daughter said, "Thanks a lot." She was afraid her son would try it, but I could only wonder how the boy hadn't already thought of it on his own.

Every time Kevin came into my house he would whistle at my parakeet Jasper, so Jasper learned how to whistle. When Kevin was upstairs working at the computer, Jasper liked to go up and sit on his shoulders. I had four collector dolls in my bedroom and Jasper liked one in particular. He would go over and sit on Sugar Plum's feet – always just the one doll. Jasper died in 2012.

Kevin went to South Korea to teach in 2001. He worked there four months and then had two months' vacation as his regular schedule. He remarried in 2006 and still works in South Korea.

Chapter 24 - Bowling and Other Hobbies

In 1963 when Fred and I lived in Girard, the young women in our neighborhood joined a bowling league. Our kids were all still in school and back then very few mothers worked outside the home so it was nice to find a reason to go out. We women enjoyed playing on that bowling league for many years.

I was living in Euclid after my husband Jay passed away. My neighbor, Mr. Pestak, asked me to join the senior bowling league with him. I bowled a couple seasons and wound up winning the first-place trophy. I quit because a lot of the people on the league were just too slow moving for me. In more recent years, I have gone bowling with my grandsons.

In 2000, Kathy Sassano asked me if I would like to go to oil painting classes with her at Lakeland Community College. We went and I enjoyed it so much we went back in 2001. I kept painting after the classes and have done 17 pieces so far. I painted two horses, two lighthouses, a mourning dove, a monarch butterfly, a waterfall, a Grand Canyon scene, an abbey on the Danube, a grey wolf, a classic house, two tigers, my homestead, a calico cat, a goldfinch and Charles Lindberg landing in Norway.

I always had an eye for and appreciated nice cars and in 2009 I was dating a retired man whose passion was classic cars. He was usually working on at least two at a time and he treated his hobby like a job. He got up early every morning to go through his regular routine and then he went out to the garage to work on the cars. During nice weather every summer, the members of the classic car group would go to designated areas, park and visit while admirers walked around and looked at the sparkling cars. Keeping them in good shape takes a lot of rubbing and polishing, and each owner, of course, wants his to be the best.

I went with Lou on several drive-through tours, and on some where everyone would just go and park. He was a very nice man. He had a turquoise 1941 Plymouth coupe and a 1939 navy blue Ford Thunderbird. He also had two other cars that he was working on.

Chapter 25 - Father

When my father was 87, he had been going to and from sons' and daughters' homes, staying a couple weeks each place. He decided he was disrupting people's lives because everyone had work and other responsibilities, so he admitted himself to a senior home that was financed by the county. There was enough land surrounding the buildings that he was able to put a garden in. Having been a farmer most of his life, this made him feel very good. He lived to be 98.

Chapter 26 - The 1990s and 2000s

In 1996, I was out walking in Geneva, and along the road I noticed a large patch of sweet clover hay. It has a delicate sweet aroma; a very clean fragrance. I gathered an armful and took it home to my basement. Last summer my niece Cheryl and I went to Punxsutawney to visit another niece. As we were out riding around, I started watching for sweet clover hay but we didn't find any. After we left I'm sure my niece Mary Lynda was out looking for some.

Later on, I had Bill take me for a ride so I could watch for some hay. We went around through the country in Geneva and Jefferson and, lo and behold, I saw two stalks. I had Bill stop and I brought it home. I have it hanging over my washer and dryer. I sent a picture of it to my niece Mary Lynda.

In 1997 I was on jury duty in Cleveland. The trial lasted 3 days. I got acquainted with three other lady jurors and we would go to lunch together. At the end of the trial, we decided to trade contact information so we could keep in touch and I was surprised when they gave me their business cards. I had no card to give in return, but I showed the cards to my friend Kevin and told him I was just as important as they were so I guessed that I needed a business card, too.

One lady was a head nurse, one an attorney and one had an art gallery. Since I was a pilot I asked myself exactly what I would put on my card and finally decided I'd put down consultant and pilot. If anyone asked what I consult on, I would just say, "You name it and we'll talk."

When I was deciding what to put on my business card, I wrote to the Federal Aviation Administration and asked them what percent of pilots were women. They responded that at present time it was 5 percent, so on my card I put 5 percenter along with pilot and consultant.

My granddaughter April was married to Patrick Copeland in 1992 and they had Taylor in 1993. Taylor was married in 2010 and she had Uriah in 2015. Jason was married in 1998, Shawn was married in 2012 and Bill's daughter Alison was married in 2012.

In 1998 I decided to move so my friend Kevin helped me look for a property. Since he was in commercial real estate, we even investigated locations for businesses. I was pretty sure I wanted to be in Mentor, so we looked at a lot of different options. We looked at mobile home parks and I considered buying a lot, but then I saw a condominium for sale that I liked at the Bellflower Terrace Development in Mentor, so I bought it and moved there in December of 1998. It had three bedrooms a bath and a half, a full basement and an attached garage. I liked it a lot. The people on my street were very friendly and I became close friends with some of them. In the summer one year at the condominium, the trimming of the shrubs had been neglected so badly the year before that they were huge and badly out of shape. I got impatient waiting for them to be trimmed, so I took my electric hedge clippers and started trimming. I worked on them for 2 days and trimmed my own and the shrubs for eight neighbors. I had large piles of clippings to dispose of at each place. I had always done my own anyway, so it wasn't that much of a strain. I still see my next-door neighbors, Kathy Sassano and Carol Witt. I helped watch my neighbor Carol's mother for a while. I would pick her up at adult day care and bring her to Carol's or to her sister Mary Jane's house.

To help out, I took Kathy's husband Gus to Cleveland Clinic for his chemotherapy when he was suffering from cancer. He passed away in 2010. I also did sewing for a few people. In 2004 I put a quilt together for a friend, Millie Hughes. In all, I made four quilts and crocheted nine afghans.

109

From 2006 until 2012, I helped plant and take care of Bill's garden in Geneva. In 2009 I took a two-inch start of a sweet gum tree and planted it in the yard at my condominium. It is now a big, beautiful tree and has such colorful leaves. In 2012 I got a two-inch start of a maple tree, which I think came from Tom and Dianna Kaneicki's tree across the street on Havenhurst Court. The tree is tall and slim, but I think it will fill out nicely given time.

In 2012, my son Bill lost his wife Pamela to hepatitis and pneumonia. Then Bill and I were devastated to learn that Terry was diagnosed with cancer. In 2015 Terry flew to Maine and bought a motor home with a lift installed so his disabled wife could travel with him, but she never went anywhere with him in it. He drove it from Maine to Kentucky and stopped at my home on the way. In 2016 Terry came to Cleveland to the Clinic to see if they could help him, but he didn't get any treatment. In September, 2017, Terry passed away and his wife passed in November that same year.

Shortly after Terry passed, his daughter April, my granddaughter, was hospitalized with pneumonia and was in the hospital for six months minus 10 days until she passed away from complications at the age of 43 on March 1.

My grandsons Shawn Potts, Jason Potts and great granddaughter Taylor Seaton and great-great- grandson Uriah Seaton all still live in Kentucky.

In 2014 I sold my condominium and bought a manufactured home with three bedrooms and two baths in a senior park. I chose the floor plan and colors and had a deck with an awning and patio added. I made my own drapes. I like it here because it is a good location, close to everything I need. The park feels like a real park because it's tranquil and has so many trees. I love my home in all seasons, but especially in the warm weather because I love to feed the hummingbirds and grow my flowers.

When I was living in Euclid we had a year that was perfect for fruit growing. The flowering crabapple tree in my front yard had such a crop of those worthless little apples that I raked them up by the bushels.

I had blueberry bushes that produced wonderful berries which I had to fight the robins to keep. I covered the bushes with wire mesh and they still somehow found a way in.

The red sour cherry tree in the back yard was so loaded with cherries that the tree looked red from my kitchen window. I had picked some cherries a couple times, but obviously not enough, because one morning I looked out and there were two big limbs lying on the ground.

I had known that at times people would prop limbs of apple trees that were too heavy with apples and in danger of breaking. I never thought that cherries could break down limbs, but these cherries were large and so plentiful that the limbs couldn't hold them. I picked more cherries from the limbs but some still went to waste. I felt very bad to lose my beautiful tree.

My retired neighbors across the street from my home in Euclid enjoyed watching me fight the raccoons that were living in my chimney. I had repaired the mortar around the top of the chimney twice, so decided to get a chimney cap. I started a fire in the fireplace to make sure all trespassers were out, then put the cap on. They were still very persistent, and kept digging at the edge of the chimney.

I also entertained the neighbors by cleaning the leaves out of my gutters. I wasn't afraid to walk around on the roof, but they got very nervous.

I have belonged to the German Club at the Mentor Senior Center for many years. We meet once a month. I also belong to a group called Cordial Connection. We meet for lunches and dinners at various restaurants. I attend the Mentor Methodist Church.

I've stated before that I enjoy repairing things. My latest project was unique. Two years ago, I bought a battery-operated snow blower that's black with a red impeller. It is lightweight, easy to take up and down steps and I don't have to bother with pouring gas. But the chute was too short, so whenever it was windy, the snow would come back in my face. I decided that I could cut out the side of a red plastic Folgers coffee container and bolt it to the chute to make it longer. The longer chute worked and I no longer had to put up with a face full of snow when I cleared my walk and driveway. The red even matches the impeller so nicely that it looks like it belongs there.

Chapter 27 - The Floods and Other Disasters

In 2006 when I lived in my condominium, there was a very bad flood that ravaged the area. It had rained for two days and there was over 3' of water in my basement. Needless to say, the furniture, carpeting and everything else down there was completely destroyed.

Because of the widespread disaster, we were compensated by FEMA and were able to replace the carpeting and furniture. Even though we were told that the area had never flooded before so it wasn't expected to happen again, I increased my homeowner's insurance to include flooding.

In 2009 it happened again. I had a $500 deductible on my insurance, and we got no help from FEMA. It's a part of life.

In 2006, my 1995 Buick Le Sabre needed a new battery cable. I left it with a local service mechanic and it was supposed to be ready to be picked up the next morning. When the mechanic didn't call, my son Bill and I went to the garage. We started the car and it shook all over. The engine was ruined.

I checked the odometer and it showed that 40 miles had been put on the car since I dropped it off. We later discovered that the manager and mechanics were both alcoholics. It appeared they had drained the oil and then took the car home for the night, which ruined the engine.

I had promised to go to Niagara Falls to see my sister June around that time, so I rented a car for 3 days. When I came back home I bought a 2003 Buick Century, which I still have.

I took the mechanic to court but he was in rehab and didn't show up in court. Somehow, that meant I lost. Figure that out!

Chapter 28 - Travels with My Friends

In 1994, June and I went to our brother Dick's place in Fort Collins, Colorado. We went camping in the mountains with Dick and LaRue. The trails were beautiful and the weather was perfect. Dick and I went panning for gold at the edge of a creek where he found a couple specks of gold, but I didn't find any. The outhouse was quite a distance from the camper, and it was very dark at night, so we would scoot over there as fast as we could with a flash light when we had to go. One morning we could see that an animal of some sort had knocked one of Dick's thermal food keepers over. We never did figure out what kind of animal had tried to raid our food supply. Dick was really good at grilling burgers, so we had a great time and full stomachs.

In 1995 my friend Norma McWherter and I went on a beautiful Scandinavian cruise to Iceland, Sweden, Norway and Denmark. It was a perfect trip. The weather was beautiful and the flowers and scenery were unbelievable.

I knew I wanted to go on a trip to Germany since that is where my ancestors came from, so in 2003 I enrolled in the first course of German language at Lakeland Community College. I started in the second course but when they got into grammar, I quit.

In 2004 my friend Norma and I went on a river cruise through Germany that was absolutely incredible. The weather was perfect and not having to move our luggage for 16 days was great. The food was wonderful and the staff was extraordinary, but we didn't need to know German, since all the people conducting the tour spoke English.

When we were in Frankfort, Norma and I wandered away from the group and suddenly realized it was close to time when we were supposed to be back at the boat, but we weren't sure which direction to go. Some teenagers came by so Norma asked them, "Which direction is the river?" They didn't understand, so I said, "Rhine" and then they knew, they said, "Yaa" and pointed us in the right direction. We made it back in time.

In 2008 I stayed at my sister June's place for three days. She always wanted me to stay longer, but I never did so she and her friends had a nickname for me - Two Day Mary. My sister had very nice next-door neighbors, Mr. and Mrs. William Brumfield. They had a big, lush green yard, and I just kept thinking how that pretty yard needed a cow in it. I thought it would be a good joke if we put a wooden cow in their yard at night so they would see it all of a sudden when they got up in the morning. June agreed because she had always liked playing jokes on people.

When I went home, I got out a large piece of wood. I had it in my living room, and was going to draw a cow on it, but then I realized what a big job that would be, so I went to several places that sold yard ornaments to try to find a cow. I couldn't find one.

I told Pam, my daughter-in-law, and she said maybe there would be something on E-bay. Sure enough, she found a beautiful cow, so I told her to order it and have it sent to June's house in Niagara Falls.

When it arrived at June's house, she and her daughter Cheryl put it in the Brumfield's yard at night. The couple was very surprised when they looked out their window the next day and saw the cow standing there. They thought it was funny, but never dreamed that June would have been the one who put it there, so they began asking the neighbors across the street from them about it. They asked several people, but no one knew who had done it.

Then they finally asked June and she admitted it. The neighbors all laughed about it and the Brumfields liked their new cow so much that they kept it in the yard and even put a fence around it. I still have a beautiful picture of it.

In 2010 I went to Washington, D.C. with my friend Kevin, his wife and his 82-year-old mother. I was also 82 at the time. We went for the Glenn Beck tea party conservative movement in government. I get involved in politics because I'm concerned about our country, our way of life and the debt that the past president doubled.

While we were there I climbed a tree on the White House lawn. It was there so I climbed it. We then went on to Williamsburg, Virginia. I had been there before but Kevin's wife hadn't seen it. There are always interesting things to see there so I certainly didn't mind going back.

In the first part of my book I mentioned that we ate dandelion greens. This is something that I have done every so often over the years when I had the chance. On April 24, 2018, I asked my friend Kathy to go with me to search for dandelions to dig so I could have a meal of them. We drove out to Geneva, but the place I thought I could get some had just been mowed the day before and it was drizzling a little rain so we went away empty handed.

I had also told my friend Janet that I wanted dandelions. The next day I went out to lunch with a friend, and when I came back there was a huge bundle of dandelions on my doorstep. Of course, I knew who brought it, but the funny part is that I didn't know dandelions were sold anywhere. Janet found it at Heinen's in Chardon and bought it. I prepared it with my mother's hot dressing and gave Kathy and Janet each a helping of dandelion greens. I have enough frozen for another meal, then I'll be ok for a few more years.

Author's Note

I am very concerned for the younger generations and the future of America, with liberal, anti-American voices speaking out and trying to destroy our way of life. I feel that technology has gone too far. It is overwhelming for the young people and we have lost our privacy. Of course, there were times when I was grateful for today's technology. In my life I have had a tonsillectomy, lapendectomy, hysterectomy, rotator cuff/shoulder surgery and five finger surgeries.

My life has been a journey of constant changes: getting electricity, a telephone, central heat, water in the house, radio, black and white television, color television, cell phones and computers. These many inventions have changed things so much and made life so much easier. I have been lucky in life. I was blessed with nine wonderful siblings and good parents. My two sons gave me a lot of pleasure.

I'm thankful for the friends and family who have enriched my life along the way. I'm fortunate that I have been able to do so many enjoyable things in my life and that I have had good health. I hope to do more sewing, more oil paintings, more organ playing, plant a lot more flowers and have some fun seeing new things and meeting new people for many years to come.

Made in the USA
San Bernardino, CA
08 November 2018